Table of Contents

INTRODUCTION

This book comes from a series of audio interviews featuring multihull designer John Marples. This audio series, also entitled, *"Knowing Your Multihull,"* was so well-received by listeners, that I began thinking about the possibility of having them transcribed, so ebook readers might also enjoy the rich multihull content contained within them. This book is the result.

Some individuals enjoy reading information, instead of listening to audios. But whichever way you prefer to glean great content, you're in for a real treat. John Marples has been a multihull enthusiast, builder, sailor, boat designer and marine engineer for over 40 years. It would be hard to find anyone more qualified to either speak about, or write about, the topics discussed in these pages.

Having said that, it's important for you, the reader, to know that any error of wording, phrasing or concept, which would have resulted from the transcription process, isn't John's fault. I've taken care to prevent such mistakes, of course. I don't know of any errors, or else they would have been corrected *prior to* publishing. So if you, dear reader, find such any such lapses within this text, then please let me know so it can be promptly corrected. Future readers will appreciate your attentiveness, and I will most certainly appreciate any helpful feedback you share with us.

It's my privilege to bring this multihull-related content to you. We multihullers love our boats. But as John says, *"They're a different animal from monohulls."* There are many points made within this publication that demonstrate that truth. And when you combine those points with the entire "general boat construction and maintenance" knowledge found in these pages, then you're probably going to possess a ton more valuable information than you had prior to reading this book.

Now, get ready to know a LOT more about multihulls! We hope you enjoy the rich, wonderful content found in this unique book.

-- Joe Farinaccio, Publisher, www.OutRigMedia.com

Knowing Your Multihull

By John Marples

Published by: OutRigMedia.com, 16 Sunset Ave., Pennsville, NJ 08070, 856-678-2186, info@outrigmedia.com

ISBN 978-0-9721461-7-3

LCCN 2014936921

www.OutRigMedia.com

Other Products Available at OutRigMedia.com...

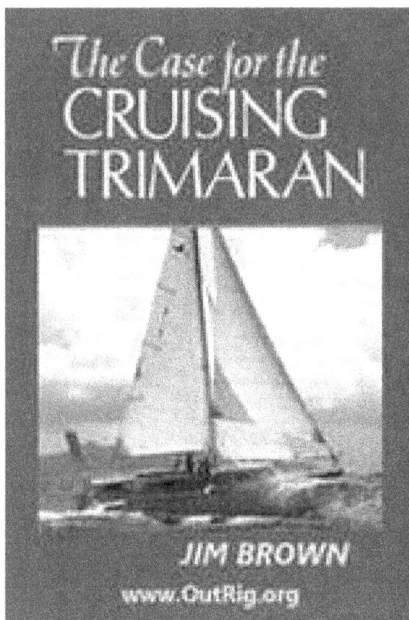

The Case for the CRUISING TRIMARAN

JIM BROWN

www.OutRig.org

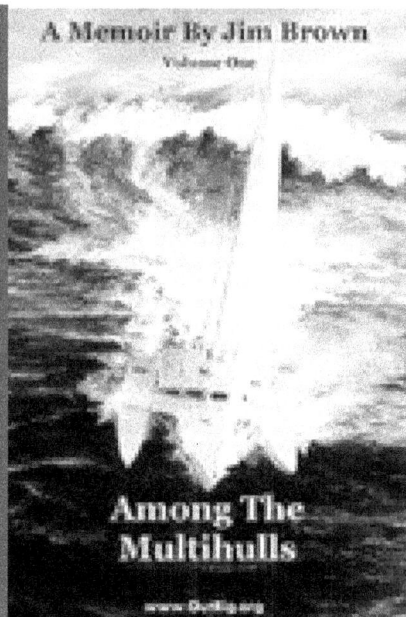

A Memoir By Jim Brown

Volume One

Among The Multihulls

www.OutRig.org

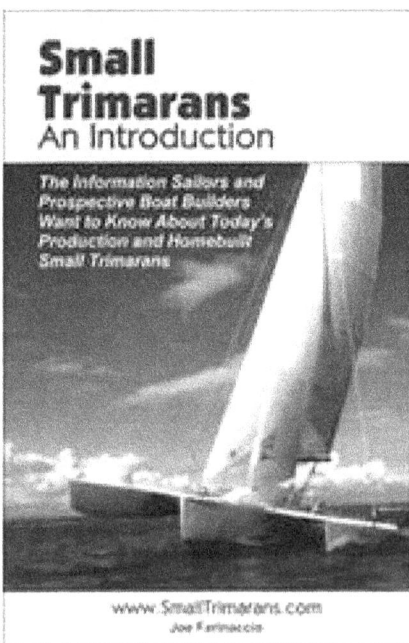

Small Trimarans
An Introduction

The Information Sailors and Prospective Boat Builders Want to Know About Today's Production and Homebuilt Small Trimarans

www.SmallTrimarans.com

Joe Farinaccio

Multihull Conversations with Jim Brown

CHAPTER ONE
DIFFERENT TYPES OF MULTIHULLS

Let's begin with a general overview of trimarans, catamarans, and proas. Each of these classes refers to different types of multihulls. And it's very important to understand that all of them are very different from monohulls.

Some of these are production boats. The majority of those we're going to look at here, however, are boats that just about anyone can build at home, either in a backyard or shop. But we're also going to look at a couple of very large, high-tech, ships. These boats include the full spectrum of what you'd expect to see in boats of any size.

Trimarans...

Let's begin with trimarans. Trimarans can be very interesting. Some people don't quite understand why trimarans exist. I always say that they're more like regular boats with training wheels,

A trimaran is, of course, a three-hulled boat. In the past, most trimarans were home-built. I see many of these for sale all over the Internet. But there are various production boats made with the latest fiberglass molding methods nowadays.

The one pictured here is a trimaran designed by Arthur Piver. Piver is the guy who is basically attributed to being the father of the modern trimaran. He put three hulls together and even designed a number of models with a livable interior. He popularized trimarans back in the 1960s.

A lot of Piver's designs are still around today. In fact, one of these old models may be the best opportunity to find a used boat for the least amount of money.

If a Piver-designed boat was properly built to begin with, has been well-maintained and ventilated, then it may be a bargain. These boats usually aren't expensive because they represent older designs. It's like buying a '58 Buick that's been in the garage for the last 30 years. It's got a lot of miles left on it, but it's not the newest thing on the block.

The next one pictured is one of my own designs – a Searunner 37. I built this one when I was 23 years old, in my own backyard. It was built out of standard plywood and lumber. All of the materials came from the local lumber yard.

I covered the hulls with fiberglass sheathing and then coated it with polyester resin. These days, the fiberglass would be covered with epoxy resin instead. Epoxy is a lot stronger.

This particular boat is still alive though. As a matter of fact, I personally surveyed it not too long ago. At the time of this writing, the boat was being enjoyed by its 3rd owner ... and it's 41 years old.

It has also sailed thousands of miles since this last survey. (This next photo was taken during my survey-examination of the boat.)

The 2nd owner of this boat had taken very good care of it. He upgraded it with a new electrical system and a recent diesel engine. He also changed out the rigging and chain plates.

The owner performed all of these changes himself. He is a technical person and understood how to do things properly. When he came across something that he didn't know how to do he called me up and used me as a consultant.

That just shows you that a 40-year-old plywood trimaran can be maintained in good shape. It's not going to rot away within the first week. This boat is ready to go across the ocean again today.

The next sketch features a familiar production trimaran ... it's designed by Ian Farrier. It's a folding, trailerable boat that's 27 feet long.

These models are among the more popular production trimarans today. They're very popular because they were a production boat.

Their value is easily established on the market because there are lots of them identically built and backed up by a manufacturer and distributors. This makes it relatively easy to get insurance for them. They're also easier to obtain financing for when purchasing. It can often be more difficult to obtain financing and insurance for older boats.

The next sketch features the Benchijigua Express. It's a 215 foot long power trimaran that serves as a freight service into the Canary Islands.

This boat can go up to 40 knots, and it's extremely efficient and features lots of deck space. It carries cars and passengers and freight.

This particular boat was really a breakthrough boat as far as transport multihulls. Until this time, multihulls in the commercial sense had not been used except for oceanographic vessels, and the Navy had experimented with oceanographic catamarans and that sort of thing. But this trimaran is really truly something different.

In general, multihulls are not known for their cargo capacity. But this boat is quite different in that regard. Multihulls are historically designed to be lighter, as speed is a big consideration.

The Benchijigua Express offers speed because the boat is large enough that the cargo weight is easily accepted by the hull, so that weight doesn't damage the performance of the boat. I was quite surprised when I first saw this boat in the magazines. The commercial shipping magazines featured stories about it.

The next sketch here depicts one of the newest vessels in America's fleet of warships. It's a Marine Littoral Combat Vessel – the USS Independence.

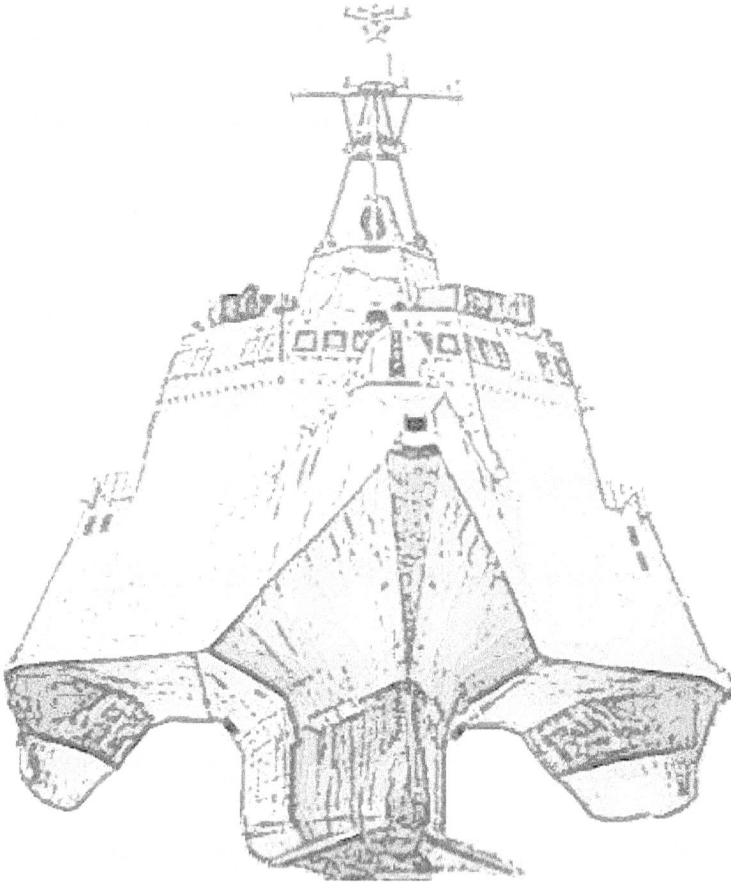

This boat carries a small platoon of Marines onboard, for fast insertion into combat areas -- probably Special Forces. It carries a helicopter, it carries a bunch of missiles and stuff, and it's a trimaran. The Navy will say this boat exceeds 40 knots; they won't tell us how fast it really can go.

This combat trimaran's existence, more than anything else, may be due to the piracy that's been occurring in places such as the Indian Ocean, off the coast of Somalia. It's ideal for chasing pirates.

This is the sixth vessel named USS Independence. It's 215 feet long and has the ability to change its location very quickly in order to go wherever the action is. That reason alone makes it a formidable piece of equipment. Imagine having a quick-response vessel, with a platoon of special forces-type warriors on board.

Catamarans...

Catamarans have been around longer than trimarans. A catamaran has two hulls that support the entire weight of the boat in the water all the time. So the catamaran is basically two hulls connected together by a series of beams. And it is very important how they're connected together.

The first catamaran here is a boat designed by James Wharram catamaran. It's different in some ways than any other catamaran design in the marketplace.

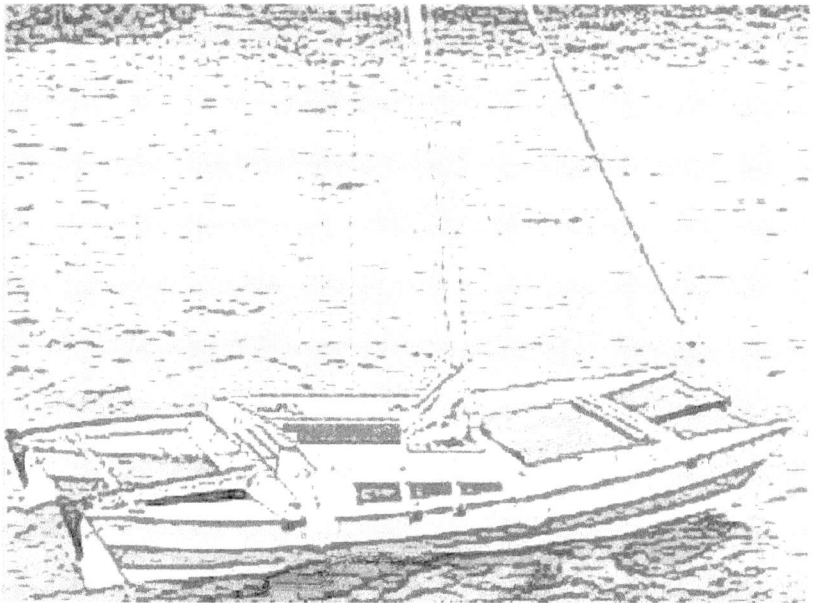

This boat actually has shock mounting on its cross beams, which connect the hulls together. This allows its whole platform structure to be flexible. Almost all other multihulls have a very rigid platform. Their platforms are essentially inflexible, except for the elasticity of the material that is used to build the boat.

This Wharram design is intentionally elastic. It reflects James Wharram's idea about what sea-going boats should be.

Wharram designs have been quite successful commercially. Thousands of his boats have been built by sailors all over the world.

In past years, they had a reputation of not being able to go to windward as well as some other designs. They were noted as being more of an off-the-wind, downwind sort of craft.

Most Wharram builders/sailors probably love these designs, however. The particular design-approach developed by James Wharram is probably one of the least expensive types of multihulls to build. That is probably one reason for their huge fan base, especially among self-builders. There are lots of other catamaran designs though, offered by many different boat designers. Many of them are geared especially for home builders.

The photo here depicts a commercial vessel. Catamarans have taken over the commercial sailing business.

When people walk down a dock and decide to go for an afternoon sale, just about anyone can look at a catamaran and say, *"Boy, that boat isn't going to heel over. It's going to be really stable. I feel comfortable with that."* They'll climb onboard, no questions asked.

This picture shows a 64-foot boat that is certified to carry up to 90 passengers. It's one of my designs.

This particular vessel operates in the Hawaiian Islands. There are lots of these types of commercial charter cats in the Hawaiian Islands. You won't find any trimarans carrying passengers for service, but you'll find lots of catamarans in passenger service.

Not long ago, a sailor attending the Annapolis Boat Show told me about some of the big, beautiful catamarans that he'd seen. They were million dollar boats. They were especially beautiful inside.

In his opinion, however, that was the extent of their real worth. He thought that while living aboard one at the dock must be like living in a beautiful hotel room, the reality is that they don't really sail too well. In other words, they looked stellar but their performance was very much lacking.

He thought many such catamarans are commercial success though. Such boats offer what many people want in the way of accommodations. And I agree that there are tradeoffs that can be considered when it comes to balancing accommodations and performance.

Many production catamaran models feature large house structures, with full interiors. They're able to offer such expansive interiors because they have a lot of real estate on deck. But one should keep in mind that a larger structure adds weight to the boat.

In catamarans, one achieves standing headroom over water with a bridge deck between the hulls. That fact alone requires those cabins to be somewhat large. In a trimaran, standing headroom can be achieved within its main, center hull without an expansive bridge deck. A trimaran's cabin structure can be lower, and since there's less of it, it weighs less.

There are other factors that can easily increase both the weight and cost of a big catamaran. Catamarans have two identical hulls in the water, which often adds a lot of duplication in terms of machinery and foils and that sort of thing. Large catamarans also require two motors and two keels, instead of one, as would be the case for a trimaran.

Large cats also have two toilets (*heads*) most of the time -- one on either side. That is because anyone sleeping in one hull doesn't want to have to get up and go to the other hull in order to go to the bathroom in the middle of the night.

Another major weight and expense factor is the rather heavy, complex beam structure between the hulls. Catamaran masts are stepped on the bridge, between the hulls, so this bridge has to be structurally quite strong.

All of these things tend to drive the weight of large catamarans way up to the point where they're much heavier than a trimaran of similar length.

In the end, there are a lot that tend to make catamarans heavier and more expensive. And the added weight may cause the performance to suffer.

Many people buying the large, commercially-built catamarans on display at boat shows don't seem to worry about whether or not they're going to have a well-performing boat. They seem to simply want something that is nice to live aboard.

Some people might think that just because trimarans have three hulls, instead of two, it means they're heavier than comparably-sized catamarans. But that's not so.

All the early French multihull racing boats, crossing the Atlantic and always trying to set new records, were catamarans. And then, at some point, someone realized that a trimaran could be a faster sea boat. They all switched to trimarans at that point.

It now seems most of the big racing boats, especially the French racers, are big trimarans. The trimarans are acknowledged to have better weather performance going upwind too. So there's been a full turnaround in that sense.

Small beach catamarans were very popular in Southern California 30 years ago. Their popularity has since waned. One can now see a lot of smaller trimarans instead.

In my opinion, I think trimarans generally excel in the smaller sizes. And as the craft gets bigger, I think a catamaran becomes the more sensible vessel to own.

Once a sailor gets a boat in the size range that offers him or her standing headroom on a bridge deck, then that is really going to be their boat of choice. This is especially true if the catamaran sails reasonably well.

As a catamaran gets bigger, the weight for its length comes down. It's more able to carry around that extra machinery and so forth. At that point, the real benefit of a large catamaran comes into play.

Again, this is my opinion, but I put the cutoff point between the optimum boat being less than 40 feet definitely in a trimaran … and being above 50 feet being definitely a catamaran. Between 40 and 50 feet? In my mind, that is a big grey area where both types of boats could work fairly well for the multihull owner.

The next photo features a power catamaran. This too is one of my designs.

It's a 54-foot boat that features a 700 HP engine; it cruises around 20 knots. This catamaran happens to be a trawler-style craft.

As you can see, it features two decks, one above the other. The upper deck is a full-width bridge that has an owner's stateroom behind it with its own bathroom. It's even got a Jacuzzi tub in that bathroom.

The deck below contains a large salon with a full galley and two guest staterooms, heads and showers. So although this catamaran is a trawler in style, it's a luxurious boat.

This craft wasn't designed to be a high-speed boat. But because the hulls are reasonably slender, the owner does get speed and a lot of real estate. This is one of the major benefits of this configuration.

This particular boat wasn't an inexpensive boat to build. The base price for a 54-foot boat like this is about a million and a half dollars. It can go up from there.

Despite that fact, there seems to be an increase in popularity for these particular types of boats. They are generally are faster than single-hull boats. They really don't take up a lot more room in the harbor. (This trawler cat that I designed is just 25-feet wide. A 54-foot boat monohull would be anywhere from 16 to 18 feet wide. So we're not talking about a whole lot of extra width. But we are talking about a lot of extra deck space on the boat and a lot of extra real estate down below.

Proas...

We've now come to another two-hulled vessel -- the proa. To many people, proas simply look like a trimaran with one of the outer hulls, or amas, being taken off. There is more to them than that though. Proas have probably been around longer than all the rest of the types of boats combined.

Proas have been used by the Pacific islanders, including Melanesians and the Polynesians, for thousands of years.

Proas are still raced in Tahiti harbor to this day. On Sunday afternoons, they have racing classes of proas.

Pictured here is what we call a Pacific Proa. The Pacific proa design carries its ama -- its outer hull -- to windward. So the righting moment of the boat is the weight of that ama, hanging out there, times the lever arm. As one can see, it's a fairly wide boat, and that outer hull hangs way out there.

This particular proa has a water ballast system built into the ama. This allows the sailor to pick up even more ballast if needed in heavy weather. The sailor can fill the outer hull up with water, giving it a lot more stability in rough seas.

Another thing about the proa design, in general, is that the boat sails both ways. By definition, a proa is a back/front boat. From amidships, going either way, it's identical. That is, it's symmetrical fore and aft.

There's a rudder on both ends, and the sails swing around so that the sails are put on the other end of the craft when necessary. In other words, a sailor doesn't "tack" a proa. They "shunt" it. In proa terminology, the "then bow" becomes the "now bow."

Shunting involves stopping the boat as it's going in one direction and then taking off in the other direction. It's hard for a traditional sailor to wrap their mind around when first seeing it. It was difficult for me.

The boat pictured happens to be built, and now sailed, by Russell Brown, who is the son of my business partner Jim Brown. Russell took me for a ride in this boat one day. He just nosed up to the dock, and I jumped on board, and he sheeted in the other sail and we sailed away from the dock going in the other direction. It was very, very strange (to me).

To be honest, I am not sure there are very many Westerners in the world that know a lot about proas. From what we do know, the proa design can be very, very efficient as a sailing vessel.

One of the neat things about a proa is its ability to just stop. Almost immediately. If you want to go from a full sail to just stopping, you can do it. The boat will just stop. And then, one can get going again pretty quickly once again.

Russell equates a proa to sort of being the motorcycle of the sea. He says it does take vigilance to sail the boat. And it should have some sort of safety valve.

On Russell's boat, one safety feature he has built into it is a pod off the center hull that hangs out to leeward. This pod actually serves a double berth inside his boat.

If Russell's proa heels too much, the pod drags in the water and provides stability. It slows the boat down and tells the sailor that they're doing something wrong. It serves as a warning that things need to be adjusted … the sails have to be reduced, or whatever, in order to safely carry on.

When a proa really gets moving, it's common for just the main hull to be in the water. Because that hull is long and slender, there isn't a lot of stress on the boat. The heeling moment tends just to lift the main hull out of the water.

A Pacific proa doesn't push its outrigger hull down into the water and create a whole lot of stress on the boat. This means proas can be lightly built. And this lightness in weight can allow them to be even faster than catamarans and trimarans of similar length. The proa is a great configuration.

One disadvantage of proas, however, is that they're not the type of boat you can short tack up a narrow harbor. That would be quite difficult; it would be a real challenge. In other words, proas have difficultly short tacking in a narrow space going upwind. Proas are best suited for open ocean work and open anchorages and so forth.

The next slide photo features a different type of proa – an Atlantic Proa. This one also goes in both directions, but the outer hull is carried to leeward, so it's live buoyancy.

This is the main characteristic of an Atlantic Proa design. It pushes its outrigger hull down into the water as it is sailing. That means its crossbeam arms have to be a lot bigger and heavier because they have to be much stronger.

This particular boat also has a safety valve. If the boat should be caught aback then it features an inflatable buoyancy chamber. This chamber can be seen alongside the windward side of it. That chamber is only there to keep the boat upright if, for any reason, the boat should be caught aback and try to capsize the wrong way.

The Atlantic Proa is really more like a trimaran with its windward hull sawn off. For long-distance races that are predominantly one tack, this type of boat was thought to be hard to beat.

The name of the boat pictured is *Lady Godiva*. It was sailed in races back in the 1980s. I don't think any recent events have had Atlantic Proas in them though. I included it here to explain the difference between the two types of proas.

I am not sure, but I don't know of an Atlantic Proa that won any significant races. I also don't know of any significant design contributions that have resulted from Atlantic Proas. Up to this point, it may be a design configuration that has been left behind.

General Differences Between Multihulls and Monohulls...

To begin with, multihulls, just by the fact that they don't carry any ballast aboard, are more shallow draft boats. This shallow draft capability, combined with a boat that will also safely go to sea, is really significant.

Having a shallow draft means there is a whole lot more navigable water out there for a sailor to explore. This includes channels and shallow areas around islands. And it certainly includes good places to hide from storms (or even hurricanes) when you're in the tropics.

Shallow draft capability also means a lot when it comes to certain kinds of maintenance. A sailor can do a good bit of maintenance work to his or her boat right on the beach in remote locations. As long as one has enough tide to get in and float the boat back out again, it's possible to beach even a large multihull in order to perform work on the boat.

I used to do all of my routine maintenance for my trimaran, Bacchanal, on a beach, whenever I could. It got its yearly scrub down and paint job and that sort thing ... right on a beach.

For a multihull owner, it's only a question of finding a spot that's good enough. I always looked for hard sand in order to careen the boat. When I did that, maintenance was easy because the boat stayed level. A catamaran would stay level under those conditions too. And so would a proa.

Once you're on the beach, you can actually arrange to set the boat's hulls on some blocking as it dried out. One could also excavate out underneath the hull to reach underwater areas of the boat. One can just dig the sand out. That's what we used to do.

We used to carry enough water with us so we could just slosh it on the hull to clean the hull of saltwater and so forth. After scrubbing a hull, we used brushes dipped in the sand that we were standing on to scrub the paint with, and then washed the sand off with fresh water in preparation for paint.

We used a hard bottom paint that dried very quickly. I used to be able to paint an entire hull so it tried and was all done between tides.

There were other times that we'd do minor damage to a hull and be able to run the boat up on a beach and repair the damage in between tides. This kind of ability gives a multihull sailor a great many more options. When it comes to performing maintenance or taking care of damage or trouble, it's often possible to do without having to find a boatyard somewhere.

The biggest challenge for multihulls, in comparison to monohulls, may be seen in their ability to capsize. By their nature, multihulls are very, very stable. Thus, many monohulls sailors would quickly add, "Yes, but only to a certain point."

Their stability gives multihulls capsize ability. Even the larger ones are known to have turned over in extreme circumstances.

Yet, here is how a multihuller might reply. Most cruising boats are heavy enough that they're very, very stable. Only in extreme survival situations would they be on the verge of capsize.

I've been out in the ocean a great many times with big, huge waves ... I've even filled the cockpit up with wave tops at certain times ... but I was never really worried about the stability of the boat.

What does have to be taken into consideration is that stability puts a great deal more stress on the rigging than it does on a keel boat. When gusts of wind hit the sails on multihulls, they don't have the strain relief of the boat heeling over. That strain relief will instead be seen in the boat accelerating. And because the rig stands up there and absorbs that wind and turns it into emotive power, that rig has to be stronger than it does on a keel boat. Many newer multihull sailors don't realize that.

A new multihull sailor might say, "Gee, this boat is lighter so it needs lighter rigging." But that isn't true. The rigging has to be substantial on a multihull boat, and it has to be properly maintained.

History reveals that dismastings weren't infrequent in earlier days of 20th century modern multihull development. It was something we learned a lot about in the 1960s and 70s. We discovered the rigging wire, in general, needs to be a little heavier on multihulls.

As an engineer and boat designer, I can assure you this reality is something that always needs to be taken into consideration. In fact, the catamaran we talked about earlier (the one that was certified for carrying passengers for hire) had to undergo the scrutiny of the Coast Guard Marine Safety Center in Washington, DC, pertaining to its design and outfitting and so forth.

The Coast Guard has its own professional engineers look over the numbers and calculations for any charter boat in order to approve them before the boat can be built. Being an engineer myself, I do that with all of my own designs. Professional multihull designers know what the loads of those shrouds are going to be, and give them plenty of safety factors in order to make sure the boat is not going to self-destruct at sea.

The thing holds true with chain plates. The chain plates, of course, are where the shrouds attach to the hull. They must be hefty enough for a multihull. All of hardware on any boat must be fit for the duty that they are designed for.

A multihull has certain stress areas and that should always be looked at and maintained. Whether you're buying a boat, performing routine maintenance on it, or hiring a marine surveyor, it's an important part of knowing your multihull.

The owner of the boat is always responsible to make sure all of that rigging wiring, including components, is in good condition. There is a long chain of components that hold the mast up. There are bolts going through the hull, holding the chain plates on to the rigging pin, to the turnbuckles to the end terminations of the cable, and the cable itself, and then on up to the top. There are pins and tangs and bolts and stuff like that.

There is a long list of things that have to be in good condition in order to keep the rig up.

We're going to go into a lot of detail about that. A multihull owner should be prepared to understand what those things are, what they do, what they should look like, and what he potential sort of problems have occurred in boats in the past.

In closing, I'll say that multihulls have been around for a long time. They're now a portion of the establishment yachting community in the Western hemisphere. They used to be considered very strange by the establishment yachting community in America and Europe, but not anymore. You now see multihulls all over the world.

CHAPTER TWO
THE MULTIHULL PLATFORM

The term "multihull platform" isn't a term that is frequently used by boat people, including sailors and owners of multihulls. It's more than a terminology, of course. When we speak of the multihull platform we're talking about an important concept that every multihull owner should understand and address to their particular craft.

Multihulls are different from monohulls. Monohulls have a single hull with a deck that's pretty much continuous from one end to the other … and no appendages hanging out. When we look at multihulls however, we can see something else. Please note the following platform stress diagram.

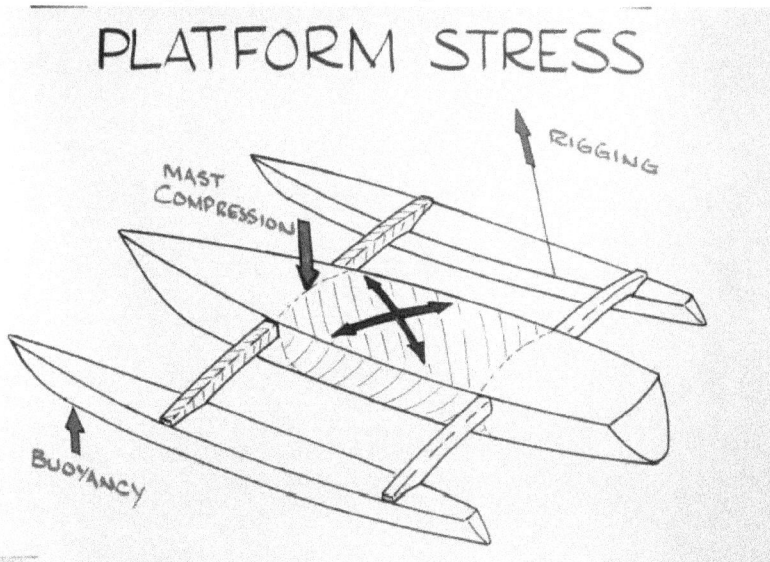

PLATFORM STRESS

I drew this diagram for the purpose showing a trimaran's platform. Catamarans are somewhat different, but a lot of this commentary still applies.

On the trimaran in this diagram, we've got a central hull -- the main hull -- and we've got some appendages sticking out. The arms sticking out are called *akas*, and the outer hulls are called *amas*.

As you can see, there are loads on all points of those various appendages. We have what we consider to be a platform. That is, a large area that is subject to being loaded in various points.

One significant point is mast compression (as you can see). That mast is pushing down in the middle area where the mast is located. The sails that drive the boat cause that mast to be loaded downward onto the hull.

Then, to support the mast, we've got rigging wire up there holding it upright. That rigging wire is pulling up on one of the amas. That pulling, consequently, causes quite a bit of stress in the entire platform. That stress ends up being shown between the two akas … the forward aka and the after aka.

The stress in these areas is trying to twist the boat. The stress is trying to ring it torsionally and pull one end from the other. This is signified by the crosses in the diagram.

That's the way the stresses go. So this this platform needs to be rigid. Many people think multihulls are designed to be flexible, as if they were all like those small rotomolded Windrider sailboats. But multihulls aren't a kind of rubber-ducky sort of thing.

There are some exceptions at times. (We're going to look at one in a moment). But most boats are made to be very, very rigid. That's the attempt anyway … a goal for rigidity.

Different Platform Designs…

In this next photo, we again see a catamaran designed by James Wharram. This boat is indeed an exception to this rigidity rule.

A lot of his catamaran designed boat may be found in harbors around the world. This one happens to be a 46-footer at sea.

This catamaran appears to have a total of four crossbeams connecting the two hulls. The crossbeam connections are bolted down through the deck using rubber washers. That allows a lot of flexibility in the deck.

The mast stays are always directly outboard. The mast is stepped on a trestle between the two forward beams, right in the middle of the boat. This allows the boat's platform to flex somewhat.

I did an experiment one day. We cruised in company with a Wharram catamaran. The owner of that boat and I got out on one of the outer hulls and started to jump up and down a little bit. We got the hulls oscillating at their natural frequency, in opposite directions to each other.

We were generating an extreme twisting situation. We got that boat to creek and crack and make some noises, and finally the owner said, *"I think we ought to stop."* He said that was weird. But he also said that while at sea that motion never occurred.

He said the boat never bobbed around with the two hulls pitching in opposite directions. Such twisting would, of course, put a lot of strain on the boat.

This sailor had gone from Barbados all the way out into the mid-Pacific on his boat. So he had quite a bit of sea-time in his Wharram cat. And in his opinion, the forces in the ocean never really caused that sort of twisting to happen with his vessel. So Wharram-designed catamarans are definitely an exception to the rigidness typically associated with multihull designs.

In the next photo, we see a standard, ubiquitous cruising catamaran. This one is about 30-some feet long.

It has two hulls connected by a rather large connecting wing, and also incorporates a cabin top. The whole structure is torsionally very rigid.

If you put a jack underneath the bow of one of these hulls and started to jack up on it, the other hull would leave the ground exactly the same time. There would be virtually no twist induced into this boat. You could not get the two hulls to point in different directions, no matter what you did.

In other words, this is an extremely rigid boat. And it's normally the case with a multihull.

Extreme Forces on Platforms...

In this next image, we see a Spronk catamaran. This is a picture of Peter Sponk's personal boat. It's a 74-foot long catamaran that's extremely slender and very, very low to the water.

This catamaran has a connecting platform, as is shown, with a whole bunch of stiffening strakes on the underside of it. You'll see why in a minute. Its platform has to be extremely strong. It takes many loads from outside the boat ... from wave tops and that sort of thing.

When boats like this are being driven hard, which is to windward ... when close-hulled and being pushed hard ... that hull you see there on the page is almost entirely immersed in the water.

The driving force of those sails is pushing the boat forward. And that tends to push the bows down into the water and lift the sterns up.

What then happens can be seen in this next photo. This shows the same boat. Notice the bow of that boat being driven -- the same bow that we were just looking at -- being driven through the wave tops here. The forward crossbeam on the boat, which holds the head stay, can be seen. And we can see the sail there just on the upper right.

Those areas are all under extreme load. Not only are the sails pushing the boat forward, but they're trying to push the boat sideways. The hull is being pushed into the wave tops sideways.

There is also a lot of buoyancy in the forward end, trying to push up on that hull, whereas the other hull is not being pushed up in a like manner. These forces are trying to twist the boat. You can also see the beam going across the bow of the boat is really quite sizeable.

Those crossbeams have to be very, very strong. They have to be anchored into the boats extremely well too.

Now let's see what it looks like at sea, when one of these boats encounters a large wave. This is a different boat.

This is boat was named *El Tigre*. It's also a Spronk design. It's about 70 feet long, or thereabouts. The photo shows it just hit a large wave. The wave smacked the underwing and the spray totally closed over the top of the boat. Everybody onboard got wet. The craft was traveling at very high speed -- probably 20 knots or so -- and after it hit that wave, its speed probably reduced down to less than 10 knots. At that point, the boat will come back down in the water and start accelerating once again.

As one can clearly see, the cross-connecting structure bridge deck between the two hulls takes some extreme loads when that occurs. It also has to keep the two hulls connected together so the boat stays buoyant.

These images show there is a lot to the multihull platform, especially when it comes to catamarans. The distance between the two hulls on a large cat can get rather wide, and because the weight is concentrated in the individual hulls themselves, that beam now has to connect those two heavyweight hulls together and keep the whole boat in one piece while those stresses are happening. Those forces can be pretty extreme.

A Need for Structural Stability...

The stresses taking place on trimarans are a little different than catamarans. The next photo here features a beautifully built, 36-foot design by Dick Newick. It has what is referred to as a "wing aka," which connects all three hulls together. We can, in a sense, consider those hulls to almost be three individual boats connected by a wing structure.

The three hulls together constitute one complete boat; but they're also all separate. In a trimaran, all the weight of the boat pretty much is supported by its center hull. The outer hulls are sized large enough so they can take the full righting moment of the sail rig, and, actually, you could stand the boat up on one of the amas, and it wouldn't completely submerge. But the outer hulls on a trimaran are never driven to that point ... except maybe in an America's Cup race like we recently saw with those large trimarans.

In a normal cruising trimaran, or even a cruising-racing trimaran, there are always two hulls in the water because that center hull has a daggerboard or keel or centerboard, and it has the rudder, and the outer hulls have none of those things.

The difference between a catamaran and a trimaran is that the catamaran hulls are rather large. If you start to capsize a trimaran, and the weather hull lifts out of the water, there's a very little bit of freeboard change in the leeward hull. In other words, the leeward hull is plenty big enough to support the entire boat without showing it very much.

As to the trimaran in our last picture, its outer hulls are sized for the correct amount of buoyancy, which would be something over 100%, over the entire weight of the boat. But the difference is, when it's being driven to windward, those outer hulls will go through the wave tops. In a catamaran, the hulls are so big they have to go over the tops of the waves.

The wave-piercing ability of a trimaran can make its ride smoother at times. Trimarans are often like a nice touring passenger car with a soft suspension. The main hull follows the shape of the seaway, and the amas just go right through the tops of the wave peaks. This can offer a smoother ride for the boat's passengers.

Having said that, a trimaran still has stress loads working on it. The mast is pushing down in the middle. The head stay and the back stay are pulling up on the ends of the main hull. The shrouds usually pull up on the amas, and the shrouds are always pulling up rather far aft.

When a trimaran is driven hard the buoyancy of the hull pushes itself up more on the forward end of the boat than the aft end of the boat. So there are a whole lot of things working together that create incredible twisting loads.

To resist those loads, we now go inside this particular boat and have a look at its structure. It's extremely elegant.

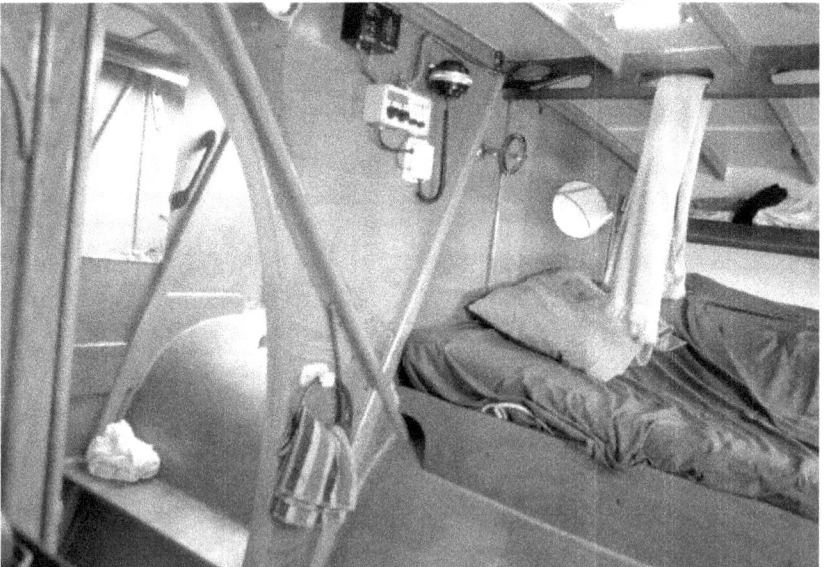

It may be difficult to understand, if you're not an engineer, but you can get an appreciation at least for what is happening. Looking inside, we see the wing that is connecting the three hulls together. What you can notice, in the lower portion of the photograph, is the actual hull of the main hull itself. The wing structure is coming from the right, and it's one complete molding. The boat is constructed of cold-molded wood and epoxy. The underwing surface rolls down and becomes the hull side ... meaning the curved portion of the plywood you see there.

What we see in this photo is a bulkhead that goes right through the boat ... in fact, two of them. We're looking through the doorway into another bulkhead, which is forward of the first one.

These bulkheads tie the underwing and the deck together to make them a really strong. The overall design results in an extremely strong structure.

There's a lot of depth to the beam, so it has a lot of ability to carry big loads from the outside without showing any deflections. And the diagonal pieces of wood there are all designed to keep that vertical plywood bulkhead from changing shape. They are present to keep things from rippling or distorting in any way ... keeping it a flat member that will carry the load. Although this is an unusual arrangement for a trimaran, it was very elegantly done in this particular boat. What we get to see by looking at it is all of the structure.

Oftentimes, structures in boats are made in sandwich bulkheads. You'll just see flat plywood in those areas. But if the trimaran is built in such a way, then it features a sandwich structure with plywood on other side. There will be a whole bunch of lumber trussing on the inside of the boat.

Twisting, Stressing Platforms...

The next image here is a sketch of the famous Oracle Trimaran. This is the boat that raced the America's Cup in Valencia, Spain.

It is 90 feet long and 90 feet wide. You can see the guys onboard there and see the scale of the boat. It's a gargantuan craft and all made out of carbon fiber.

Its three hulls are connected together by two, relatively small, wing beams. This image looks a lot like the previous image, where we saw the trimaran's platform stress.

The important thing to note here is that if you look very carefully, there's some significant twisting going on in this boat. You can see the leeward hull on the left there is riding fairly level in the water. And then the windward hull, which is flying quite high above the water, is actually pointing down.

The twisting is happening even though this boat is entirely built out of carbon fiber. It was designed by some very high-powered engineers to take the loads that are being imposed on it. And even so, from what I'm told, they had sensors all over this boat, measuring stresses and so forth, and coming back to a main computer so that the helmsman could be warned if he was going to break the boat.

Even in a world-class boat like this, if one puts too much load on it the craft will break apart. I've heard that by the big races, the engineers of this trimaran discovered that the sensors were telling them that they were very, very close to the breaking loads on the boat almost all the time.

For a boat such as this, it's actually what they wanted. They wanted to reach for peak performance with regards to the efficiency of the structure. They wanted to get as close to the ultimate loads as they could. They were very careful about building this boat too heavy because they didn't want the craft to always go slower than it could otherwise.

Pushing a boat like this for racing purposes if one thing. That's about the only time you'd ever want to approach the stresses of the boat in that manner. They were always prepared to go all out.

In this image, we see the same boat from a different direction. You can see what the rig is doing to this boat.

You can leeward hull, in the far background there, in the water. The transom is in the water. The main hull has its transom up out of the water. The rudder on the main hull is only half immersed. The hull that's closest to us actually has a downward angle to it. You can see a significant twist occurring in the entire platform.

That twist is something the racing team was willing to accept. It doesn't hurt the performance of the boat. They did everything that they could to possibly reduce the amount of this twist. But this is what they had to live with. In a perfect world, there would be no twist in the boat. But in order to get the boat to accept the stress from the sails that are being imposed on it, there has to be some deflection.

Stress causes deflection, and that racing team lives with it. So that shows us what the racing boat side of things looks like.

Design & Buoyancy...

The next photograph here shows of one of my 44-foot trimaran designs at sea. In fact, I took this photograph on a delivery of this boat as we sailed back from Hawaii quite some while ago.

As noted, this is a 44-foot long boat and it weighs about 12,000 pounds. The photo shows us going along, lickety-split ... sailing to windward. We're going north of Hawaii, travelling due north, into the Pacific, on our way back to San Francisco.

The waves got a little bit choppy out there, and the boat was being pushed hard. You can see that we'd just pushed through a wave top there. That's the ama on the left and main hull on the right. I'm sort of cowering behind the dodger because there was a lot spray on the boat.

We were moving pretty fast ... probably moving 13 to 15 knots. The boat was really making good time. But it got wet for us. That's just the nature of the beast. I mean, we were down very close to the water.

That forward aka, which can be seen (with the orange arm sticking out there), is actually a sort of triangular shaped. The bottom of the triangle is almost level with the water line, and the top is angled down so there's sort of a wave-cutting angle. The leading edge of the wing is pointed.

As we drove the boat forward, we would clip off the wave tops with this cross-connecting structure there. But that didn't slow the boat down. And that is my point here.

You can see that as the aka goes outboard there, it reduces in height. You can also see that the aka itself goes into the ama hull through the deck and not through the hull side. And that means the entire hull is available for buoyancy.

We could drive that thing right down into the wave tops. We cut the wave tops off, but didn't drag anything in the water … unlike that big Spronk catamaran we saw previously (the big yellow catamaran that had the low underwing clearance.)

That Spronk-designed catamaran had all those ribs and everything underneath it to support it. It would drag through the wave tops and slow the boat down in similar conditions at sea.

One other benefit of a trimaran is that distance between its two hulls is significantly shorter. The trimaran would overall probably wider than a catamaran of the same length, but the individual distances between its hulls is much shorter. That helps make its platform stiff and a lot easier to accept the stresses imposed by the rig and the waves and everything else. The stress is delivered to the main hull which is the main structural piece.

Design & Structural Integrity…

The next image is a sketch of a very well-known racing trimaran. This one is 105 feet long. It holds the world's record for an around the world trip with a crew … at 57 days, I believe. They left France and went down through the South Atlantic. They went around Antarctica and sailed all the way around the world -- at least around all of the meridians -- and then came back up the Atlantic to finish back in France again. They did that in 57 days, which is quite remarkable.

This boat displays a typical racing trimaran configuration. The hull is extremely tubular, with no wing extensions. The akas are the same sort of wave-cutting shape as the previous racing boat we looked at, so they can just push through the wave tops.

This very large boat has just two akas holding the whole thing together. The significant thing here is that those two akas are attached to the main hull. There are no penetrations through the main hull. There is no cockpit in between the beams either ... it's behind the after beam. The hull and deck are continuous between the crossbeams -- the hull is uninterrupted -- which means the torsional rigidity of the boat's platform is significantly improved.

I often use the analogy of a shoebox when I'm taking about how rigid we can make things. If you take just a regular shoebox, glue the top on, and then put your hands on either end and try to twist it in order to destroy it, you'll discover it's extremely rigid. It's very, very, very strong.

The difficulty with boats is that you always have a tendency to want to cut cockpits and things into the top of the box. Us boat designers have to accommodate the people that live onboard these boats. So we start cutting holes in the top of the box, which allows the platform to start twisting a bit. But if that happens too much then one will find out that, at some point, there is considerable flexibility induced into the shoebox because you're taking away one of the main structural members of the boat, which is the deck.

The racing multihulls are therefore very, very careful with how they arrange their structures. In the larger boats, it happens that one can make the entries into the hull totally separate from the highly-stressed connective areas of the hull between the two akas. It's very important. And here, on this particular boat, you can see the mast is almost perfectly right in the middle, between the two akas.

The compression stresses of that mast are now shared by the two beams, instead of being mainly on one beam. In fact, the forward beam is considerably further forward on this boat than it is on most race boats.

A part of the reason is the bows on those amas. They're big, long cantilevered things. The other hulls are able to hang way out there because of the strength of those amas.

Boats like this one go airborne. Right now, in the image we just looked at, I would guess that the boat is doing 25 knots. That is, in fact, the speed they averaged going around the world. It is incredible.

Even though I don't design racing boats, and most multihull sailors aren't going to own a boat such as this big racing trimaran, all of these factors need to be considered with regards to the design of every multihull. It's just easier to explain when we skinny-down the structure and just see a bare skeleton of a boat, such as these race boats, than it is when you see a full-winged cruising boat with a full cabin onboard.

It's just so much easier to explain these concepts using these images of racing multihulls because you can easily see all the individual components hanging out there.

Unacceptable Engineering...

In the next image sketch, we see somebody's idea of what would be the cheapest, aluminum trimaran ever conceived. This is a boat called the Tin Can.

I've included this boat to illustrate the fact that not all boats have an engineering background associated with them. I can assure you that this boat wasn't successful at all, for reasons we'll now discuss. But the fellow who built this thing must have spent a tremendous amount of money on a concept that wasn't backed up by any engineering calculations. It always amazes me how much money people are willing to commit on ideas that are not well-based.

To be more specific, I am sure this boat sails. It may even go fairly fast because it is very, very slender, and it's not very heavy. But the absolute flat bottom, from one end to the other, is going to create tremendous steering difficulties for the boat. The boat is not going to want to turn corners … it will be very difficult to get it to turn.

As we can see in the next image here, the stresses of the twisting platform in this particular boat are all concentrated at this one point right below the mast. If you can just imagine this boat, on a smaller scale, and grabbing the akas, one in one hand and one in the other, and you gave it a good twist. You can easily imagine all that pipe structure there just twisting and deforming very, very easily. One could just break the boat apart.

In fact, that is just what started to happen. I'm surprised the builder of this thing actually got this far. This is outside the Golden Gate, going into the Pacific. He did turn the boat around after he started to be alarmed at the way the structure was performing. The boat was twisting and it looked like it was going to twist itself apart. He turned around and came back.

The previous photo was taken of the boat on the ground, after the sailor had returned. I'm not quite sure what his plans for it are at the moment. The boat could be repaired. The first thing to do would be to install two crossbeams, in the same configuration we've seen in the race boats. One at the forward going directly across the boat, and one aft, going directly across the boat, connecting all three hulls together. That would solve the main problem. It would be the main thing to do in order to prepare the boat to go off sailing again. So this boat serves as a good illustration of unacceptable engineering.

Particular Boats, Specific Services...

The final image here is of a boat named *Trilogy II*. It's a 64-foot catamaran. This is one of my designs.

Trilogy II is one of the catamarans I've designed for a particular charter carrier in Maui, Hawaii. It's a molded wood boat. It's got a great big cabin structure. And it's certified for exposed water surface service. That means it can carry passengers, between islands and beyond, 20 miles for safe harbor of refuge. It's certified to carry up to 90 passengers.

Boats such as this typically have long, long lives. They're well-maintained, well-ventilated and extremely strong.

We have to design them to an accepted standard of structures. In my case, I refer to the American Bureau of Shipping, offshore racing yachts or plastic reinforced vessels. I do stress calculations for the structure to prove it is going to hold together.

Trilogy II is a 40,000-pound boat, so it's not a lightweight in any sense. It's probably analogous to a school bus, whereas the racing boats we've discussed in this chapter are analogous to Formula One race cars. They're very different animals. They do have the same sort of structural cross-tying between the two hulls as the race boats. There's a big main beam we call the forward aka, which goes across the boat at the forward end, and then another one in the aft end of the boat. Then there's a cabin structure that pretty much bridges between the two. It creates a huge, tubular structure over the boat that adds significant rigidity to it. There is always a concern about a catamaran such as this, however, because it features two 350 Hp diesel engines on it. It can go over 20 knots just with engine power.

One could waterski behind this boat. You could have a dozen water skiers behind this boat because the boat is not only used for sailing excursions, it's used to transfer passengers between two destinations. It often delivers a load of passengers and then goes back and picks up another load of passengers and ferries them back and forth. So it does ferry service along with sailing service. It is also set up to do dive service, so it's got a lot of equipment on it for diving with tanks and so forth. It's well set up to do a whole number of things.

This boat is made to the job the owner needed it to do. The fellow I drew up the plans for wrote a very complete specification for exactly what this boat was to do. And that specification varied considerably from the race boats we've seen the pictures of and from the cruising boats we've seen pictures of previously here. So each boat has a service for which it is designed specifically, generally. There is no general boat you just modify in order to make it do this or that. Boats are specifically designed to do a purpose.

In Summary...

Unlike monohulls, which have a finite amount of room in which to load on more gear and more stuff, multihulls often seem to have unlimited room. They often feature large cabins, big airy spaces and lots of room inside the hulls.

The hulls get quite large because they're tall. There is standing headroom down below on these boats, most of the time, if they're over 50 feet. This means the boat can become quite heavy. But this weight really contributes to some of the platform stress.

The extra weight that can build up on a multihull due to overloading isn't a part of the boat's design. The boat was designed to be a particular weight. As designers, we have a difficult time telling people not to cram all of the compartments full of junk.

I've been aboard boats that have been jam-packed with stuff. Some of those boats were more than 50% over their designed weight limit. They still sailed long distances, and the boats were able to make those journeys. But at some point, overloading will begin creating damage.

Remember that a multihull basically has to ride on top of the waves. It has to stay above the wave tops. That's the whole plan. As a multihull gets heavier, its response to the shape of the seaway gets more sluggish. Pretty soon, it's not climbing over the waves; it's smacking the wave tops really heavily and laboring. And those loads from wave tops really pound the bottom out of the boat … the bottom of the underwing that is. The pounding can eventually do considerable damage.

So that's a real problem with a multihull. If it's overloaded and accumulates weight beyond its ability to carry that weight in conditions the boat was originally designed for then structure damage can occur.

The bottom line for a multihull owner is don't overload the boat. That's been our mantra for a long time.

Some designs are less forgiving than others. Designs in the racer category are very sensitive to weight. Most of their sailing life will be spent racing around buoys.

In my opinion, the smaller Farrier trimarans would fall into that category. They are among the more popular production trimarans today. But they shouldn't carry a lot of weight. It's just too easy to overload those boats.

Other multihulls that have more payload capacity would let them be loaded up a bit more. But that is one thing that a prospective buyer should really look into before they consider purchasing a used boat.

Find out what its original use was. Find out what its original weight was supposed to be. Learn what its design weight was supposed to be and then find out also how much it weighs now in order to get an idea as to what sort of payload is left on the boat.

One often sees a multihull just sitting at the dock, with no people or anything aboard, and the boat is right up to its maximum displacement. Its payload is already at capacity. Such boats are heavily compromised in their sailing ability, especially in a rough seaway.

This is one reason you should always get a boat surveyed before buying it. One of things I do as a surveyor is determine whether the boat is fit to provide the service for which it was designed.

CHAPTER THREE
STRUCTURAL LOADS AND MULTIHULLS

All boats have loads coming at it from various directions. Let's discuss the concept of loads a little bit further.

The first load we can mention is the hydrostatic load. This is the load that supports the boat in the water. The water is pushing inboard on the sides of the hull, and the hull is resisting that and creating buoyancy to keep the boat up.

The boats we're talking mostly about here, sailboats, have got masts and rigging and all sorts of things that create additional loads when the boat is sailing. The lift caused by the sail, or the wind flying over the sail rather, creates a load that tries to capsize the boat. That load is resisted by the rigging wire and by the mast pushing down on the boat, etc. So there are loads from all different directions.

In multihulls, structural loads become even more complicated because, in one sense, each of its hulls can be seen as an individual boat. A multihull then, depending upon whether it's a proa, catamaran or trimaran, has several boats in the water.

In the case of a trimaran, there are "three boats" in the water. Each one carries a different sort of load and causes strain on its platform. This is why we first talked about the concept of platform in the previous chapter.

Engineering At Work...

Let's start off by looking at a little diagram that I've labeled stability. It shows basically a trimaran, or you can see, actually the weather hull dotted so that it could be an Atlantic Proa, but it's not dissimilar to a catamaran, either.

STABILITY

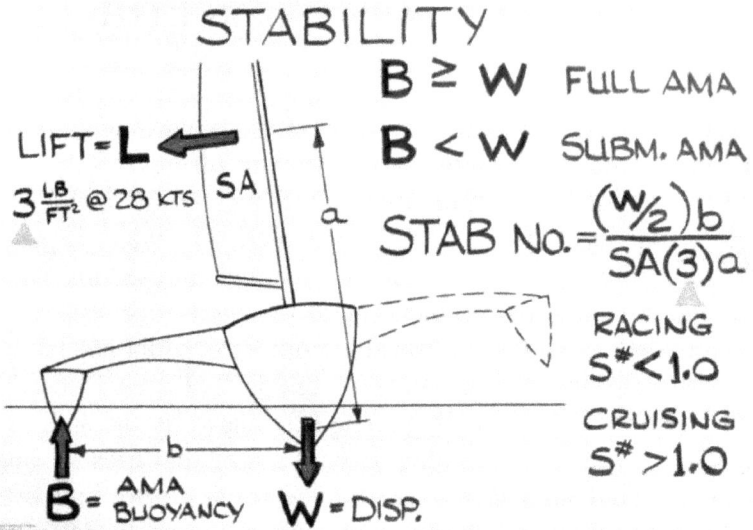

$B \geq W$ FULL AMA

$B < W$ SUBM. AMA

LIFT=**L**

$3 \frac{LB}{FT^2}$ @ 28 KTS   SA

$$STAB\ No. = \frac{(\frac{W}{2})b}{SA(3)a}$$

RACING

$S^* < 1.0$

CRUISING

$S^* > 1.0$

$B = $ AMA BUOYANCY $W = $ DISP.

What you see in the illustration is just the load caused by the sail performing its function and creating lift. And that force is trying to capsize the boat in one direction. But then the ama hull on the other side is creating some buoyancy resisting that.

What we're going to talk about here is the inner connection between these hulls and how those beams, we call them *akas*, resist all of those loads. We're going to take a look at how it's done and, in some cases, how poorly it's done.

We can now go to the next photograph which shows a trimaran on a beach. As previously noted, the ultimate demonstration of a multihull's stability is seeing the boat sitting on the beach. It doesn't fall over. It stays reasonably level because there is more than one hull connected by beams.

I personally like referring to the beams as akas. I used to call them crossbeams, but from a designer's standpoint, writing out crossbeam on the drawings all the time was laborious. So I adopted the word *aka*, which is the Polynesian term for the crossbeams between the hulls.

I refer to the crossbeams as akas for all multihulls. The Polynesians, in fact, used catamarans more frequently than they used other types of boats, including single outriggers (proas). So the term covers the main structural bulk heading that goes between any two hulls.

In the case of the trimaran, that aka goes through from one side of the boat to the other. It's the same structure, and so it attaches to all three hulls. But we only need to examine that one side at a time in our discussion here.

And you can see in my next illustration, I've put on a note that says "calculate the stress here or strength here." If we equate to a person standing there with, say, some weights in their hands, and their hands stretched out sideways, you can see that the main hull represents the body of the person. That first "calculate strength here" arrow points right to the armpit or the shoulder.

AKA STRENGTH

$$① \ M = B\ell$$

CALCULATE
STRENGTH HERE,

$$② \ M = Bf$$

$$\sigma = \frac{Mc}{I}$$

$$I = \frac{bh^3}{12}$$

B

ℓ

B

AKA SECTION

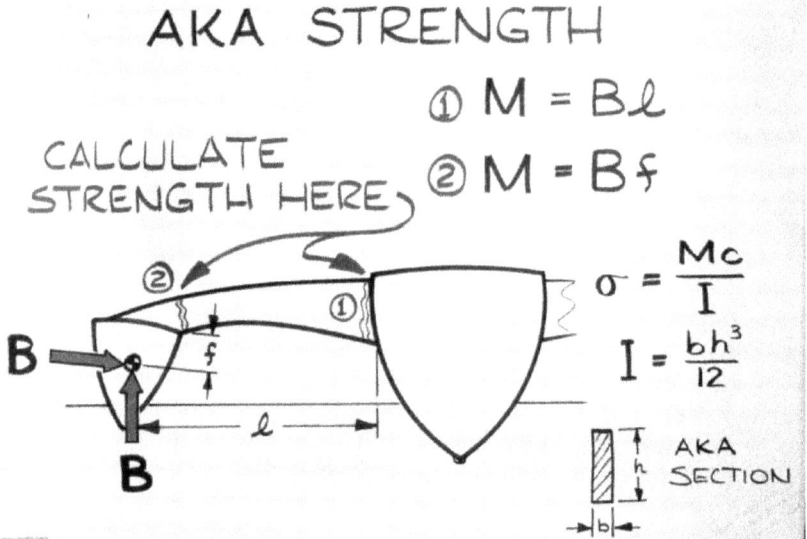

The second one points to what would be the wrist on your body. And that's what we call them. Those beams are cantilever beams, and catamarans are a little bit different. They're not quite cantilevering, but for all intents and purposes, they're basically the same.

A cantilever beam has strength, as this diagram shows, by the third power of its height. That is its vertical depth from, say, the deck to the underwing. Those terms on the right-hand side are engineering terms to describe how the beam is constructed and what sort of strength we can expect out of it.

Obviously, if you had a 36 foot boat and you attach the amas with just 2 x 4s, it's not going to be enough. But if you stacked up a lot of 2 x 4s, one on top of another so that they could become quite thick, it would do the job very well. So there's an optimum size of beam in there that will do the job properly, and that's the attempt we're trying to illustrate here with these simple engineering equations in order to determine what that beam looks like.

Structures Versus Loads...

Crossbeams can get complex, and they function in different boats different ways. We can see the next image here.

This is one of my 40 foot trimaran designs. You can see that the aka is entirely enclosed by a deck structure and an underwing structure. But there's a beam in there nevertheless. There's one forward and one aft. That's the normal arrangement for these beams in the multihull boat. That beam enters the ama through the deck, which means that it has to be shaped or attached to the ama in such a way that the strength of the attachment point isn't compromised.

You can see in our illustration that it's quite deep. The area where that beam is going to be is quite deep, adjacent to the main hull there, and it gets more slender as it goes outboard to the ama.

A more mechanical demonstration is shown here in this next illustration, which depicts a popular production trimaran model. This one has three hulls. But it's noted for having a folding system in it. The amas, or outrigger hulls, fold up next to it for the purpose of making the boat easy to trailer.

We can see underneath the boat, adjacent to the main hull, there is some diagonal structure there that is part of the folding system. But that structure also creates a lot of strength, at the point where it attaches to the main hull.

We can also see the distance between the top of the beam and the bottom, where that structure attaches, is much wider. It's a greater distance than the thickness of the beam, where it attaches into the ama. That is because the ama is basically resisting sideways forces. When multihulls are sailed hard, they often leap out of the water. Then they slam sideways into the next wave, and that wave tries to roll that ama inboard toward the main hull.

The force is pretty severe. I've been on boats that have gone airborne and done that. The force creates a huge splash and lots of spray, and you wonder how far you can go before you break the boat.

The attachment in the main hull, at the main hull, is much easier to define because the buoyancy of the ama is a fixed amount. It has a definite distance away from where it's attached to that hull. You can define that strength requirement in terms of a moment, that is a force times a distance, trying to break that thing off. And it's easy to calculate that and then build a structure that will resist the forces it has to handle.

In our next image here, we're looking inside the Newick-designed trimaran once again. We looked at this boat in the previous chapter about the multihull platform.

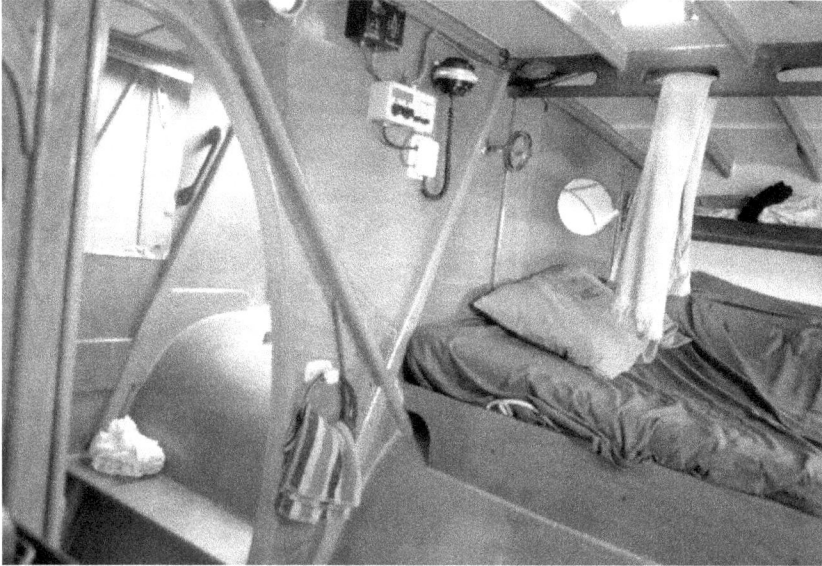

The bulkhead structure in this picture makes a whole lot more sense to us now because it is basically an I-beam construction. An I-beam was designed long ago. It is a beam that has a section that looks like an "I" with a flange on the top and a flange on the bottom with a web in the middle.

If you try to bend an I-beam, you support the ends of it and put a load on the middle and you try to bend it down into a curve, it starts to become apparent that the material on the bottom of the flange has to elongate. It stretches; it's in tension. And conversely, the material on the top flange is going to be pushed together or be in compression. And then the material in the middle sort of holds the two flanges apart, and the amount of load in there is only significant where it attaches into the flanges and holds the two flanges with respect to each other.

Here in this boat, we can see we've got the perfect situation. We've got an aka composed of a flange on the top, which is the deck -- a rather large flange in fact -- and a flange on the bottom, which is the underwing of the boat. Then this web in between them, which has a bunch of pieces of lumber on it, makes it very stiff, so it can't distort out of shape. It can't buckle and deform. And that creates a very, very strong aka structure that resists bending very well.

Basically, this shape here is taking place where the traditional beams are that we see on most trimarans. This particular multihull features those two aka bulkheads you see inside of it, and they're fully decked between them, and the underwing goes between them. Then it fares up into a point at the leading edge there. It's something Dick Newick called a "wing aka." And it looks like a single structure. This wing aka has a number of bulkheads inside of it though.

Structures Ready for Pounding...

Our next image here shows that aluminum trimaran we've previously discussed called the *Tin Can*, which was designed by its owner. Once again, we can see it illustrates some of the mistakes one can make in designing akas. This boat has two akas, and they cross each other right in the middle of the boat, which is the first mistake. As we've explained in the platform section, this flawed design offers no platform rigidity at all.

Secondly, it's got a tube on the top and a tube on the bottom, which is used for each one of those akas. They're spaced apart by bunches of other tubes that go vertically in between. But because that aka right there is supposed to take some uploads from its outboard end there, we can see that all of those spaces in between those uprights can deform into a parallelogram. The whole thing is going to fail from bending. It needs some diagonal pieces to hold all of those rectangular spaces to keep them in the shape of rectangles rather than parallelograms.

In the case of this flawed design, there's a lot of bending on those upper tubes. It's sufficient to say here that whole structure is inadequate. It's obvious that the fellow who designed it didn't have any understanding of engineering principals.

The next image, once again, shows us Peter Spronk's 74 foot catamaran named *Checha*. It has a really large wing deck that forms the platform in between the two hulls to stop the two hulls from twisting.

Now we can look at how that beam is also rather deep, and as such, it's rather low to the water. I've always felt that is a design fault. Having said that, this boat goes fairly fast. But that beam has to be very, very deep, because those individual hulls are long and slender. They're rather deep in the water, and there's a lot of twisting motion on the hulls trying to break them off and roll them together ... meaning, roll the keels together when the boat is being sailed hard.

The next image here can give us an appreciation of seeing spray when the bow is immersed so deeply in the water. One can easily imagine the tremendous loads on those beams across the boat.

One thing about these wooden boats we've looked at is that they're built with epoxy. The epoxy bonds the wood together in such a way that the boats aren't going to creak and crack. They don't do anything like that because there aren't any parts that can move with respect to each other. But they can deform!

There's some bending going on there that we don't see in the picture. The loads on those beams are significant.

The next photo shows one of my 44 foot designs. In fact, I think I took this picture at sea, while driving the boat hard. You can see that the ama is almost flush down into the water. There's spray coming up, and we can look at the forward aka there.

We can see it's fairly wide right, adjacent to the main hull on the right-hand end. On the left-hand end where it dives into the deck there, there's a considerable hump in the deck. That hump is there to keep the section of that aka really big at the point where it attaches to the ama hull. It gives it significant strength.

Big Racing Multihulls, Bigger Loads...

In the next sketch here we see a boat called *Groupama*. It's a 105 foot long racing trimaran and we've already talked about how it set an around the world speed record at 57 days. It sailed from a port in France, went all the way around the world, and came back to the same port in France. Its average speed was 21 knots.

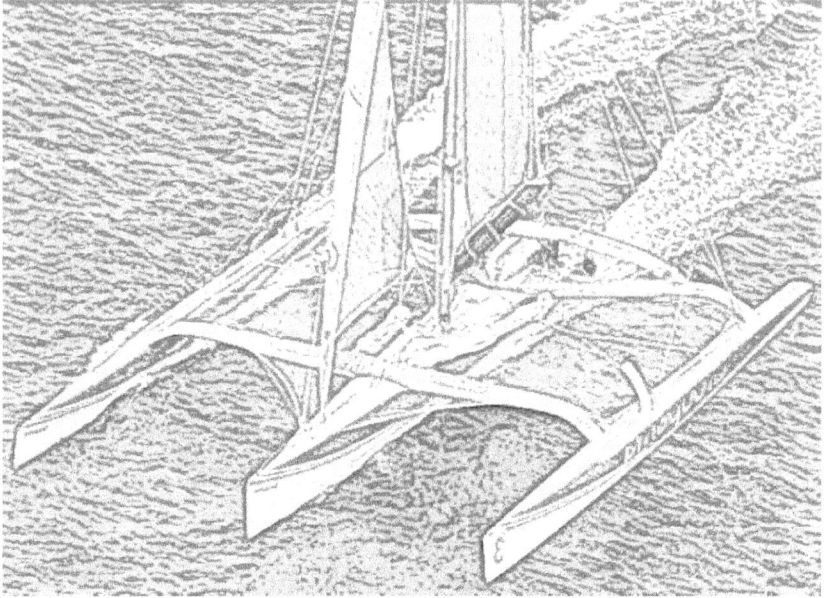

To achieve that average speed, this trimaran must have been going over 40 knots for long periods of time. It's incredible!

We can take note of the fact that it's a spindly boat. It's got two main akas connecting the three hulls together. As I mentioned in the platform chapter, there are no holes in the main hull between the two akas for strength reasons.

On the weather side-- in this image, the left-hand side of the boat -- we notice that it's got a curved daggerboard coming up out of the ama. That daggerboard is in the up position, on the windward side. On the leeward side we don't see the daggerboard because it's all the way down. The point here is that board is a foil that is pierces through the water.

In this next sketch we have a better view of it. This is the ama that shows that board coming up. We can get an appreciation for the size of the boat here from the size of the sailor standing on the floor deck. At 105 feet long, it's a big monster of a boat. It takes a lot of manpower to sail it.

The daggerboard we're looking at stops the boat from going sideways. As such, it puts tremendous twisting load on that ama hull.

In *Groupama's* first record attempt, it actually broke one ama off at the ends of the akas, right where they attach into the hull. The daggerboard itself caused a failure in the hull; the hull split open. And then, of course, it filled with water and eventually broke off. The outrigger hull was damaged ... it probably suffered a compound fracture from one end to the other.

In this next sketch we see *Groupama* being lifted down from the container ship that saved it in the middle of the Indian Ocean where their breakdown occurred. It reminds us that aka strength is a really important part of the engineering of a multihull. Of course, this isn't the first boat to have difficulties with respect to strength in its members.

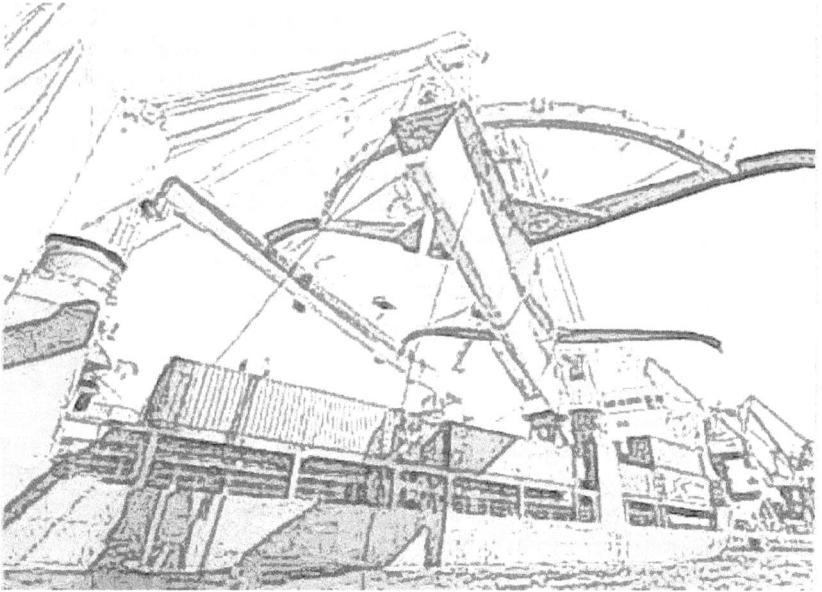

Some guys who build their own multihull by using a designer's plans think it's possible to alter the design of the boat designer. If they're not engineers with lots of marine experience, I would discourage that. You see, if a designer is qualified, you really don't want to make any changes on their design because they've gone to the trouble of figuring out where all the loads are going to be and how the structure should be made in order to accommodate the pressure and the force that is on the parts of this platform. Any changes will alter the design ... it's just not a good idea.

You might expect a designer like me to say that, of course, and there are some guys who can get away with modifying their boats. Some guys get away with hot-rodding them, putting bigger sail plans on the boat, lengthening them out or doing other things. But what you find out is that one change telegraphs right on through the boat and creates the need to change other things, which creates the need to change other things. And then it's a long chain of changes. I've had buyers of my boat plans call me up and say, *"Gee, I want to build one of your 35s, but I want to stretch it out to be 38 feet long. Can you do that?"* I'll tell them right off, *"We can, but I'd much rather start with a clean sheet of paper."*

It's much easier to begin a design with a clean slate because one finds out that when they make the boat longer, it then ought to be wider. And then when it's wider, well, the akas aren't strong enough; they've got to be bigger too. And so, as I said, it just telegraphs right on through the structure and gives a designer nothing but fits.

This has happened in too many cases with boats. Sometimes a builder can get away with it and sometimes they can't.

Multihulls Can, Literally, Be Driven to Destruction...

The next illustration features a commercially popular, plastic folding trimaran once again. The same one we talked about in the previous chapter.

The reason I'm showing this again is because we want to look closely at the next photo, which shows an ama broken off.

It suffered from an issue much like Groupama, that big racing trimaran, suffered from. In this case, it has happened on a smaller scale ... one that any of us could encounter when sailing. I don't know the background story behind this failure, but it does illustrate that at some point, if push comes to shove, there is a potential failure point right there. The potential forces exerted in these areas need to be treated very carefully by a boat designer.

Another thing to point out is that even if a boat has been properly engineered, under the right conditions, it can still fail. I've often said that it is very, very difficult to drive a monohull keel boat to destruction because you've only got so much riding moment to deal with. Also, the boat will only go so fast. If you overstretch it, it just lies flat in the water and wallows there until you do something and let it back up again. But the multihull is a different animal.

A multihull can, literally, be driven to destruction. I've had my Searunner 37 trimaran airborne a number of times ... a couple of times when I was surfing waves with it, not very intelligently, off the California coast. I've done it more than a few times at sea, in fact, when the boat was going very fast, in very steep seaway. We'd be blasting along and everything would be fine, and all of a sudden I'd look out, and everywhere I looked, we were on top of this great big wave, and the water was going down from where I was standing. The boat had just leaped off into space. It became airborne, and when it came back down into the water, it slammed down with a lot of noise … and a big jolt.

I was doing that with just a home-built plywood trimaran. And the boat could have been driven to destruction. Fortunately, I didn't destroy it. I did do damage to it a couple of times, by pushing it too hard. But one must realize that it's not hard to push these boats to the point where damage does occur.

Crossbeam Strength…

In this next photograph here, we see a Dragonfly 33. It's a very beautifully designed, folding boat. It's has a swing-wing folding system, where the amas swing inward to the main hull.

In the next image we can see the hinging mechanism on the Dragonfly's ama deck. There's actually a turntable and a big pivot pin and a whole bunch of structure. You can see that there is actually a waterstay that comes from the main hull and attaches into the aka, right there at the ama junction, to give it more stability.

That whole thing swings fore and aft and condenses the boat down, as you can see in the next picture here, so that you can put it in a slip. When this trimaran is sailing, the boat is over 20 feet wide, and when it's folded up like that, it looks like it's maybe less than 10 feet wide.

I'm not sure what the exact dimensions are, but it gives the boat a significant advantage. All of the hulls sit on their own water lines. The difficulty for this boat was that it had been tied on the dock during a storm. The wave forms in the harbor got a little bit steep and there was some heavy chop in the harbor. As a result, the boat bounced up on the dock; the ama was actually climbing up on the dock.

As a result, the crossbeams were damaged because the beams weren't really designed to carry a lot of load in their folded condition. The pounding on the dock did some damage to the metalwork and hinging mechanisms. That was one area where one wouldn't normally think that they'd need to spend a lot of time worrying about. So it goes to show that one has to look at the boat in all possible conditions of its existence. In this case, the owner needed to be concerned about the boat even when it was all folded up.

The following photograph shows a small, 24-foot sailing trimaran named *Magic Hemple*. This boat won the around Britain race many years ago. It's quite a grueling race, taking boats all the way around England and Ireland, offshore, in some very nasty, choppy water and some fairly nasty conditions. I think the race is conducted in a number of different legs. And this boat did extremely well.

Even though this boat is only 24-feet long, it has got a 40-foot mast on it, with a giant rig. It was sailing Swift Shore Race, off Port Townsend, going up the Strait of Juan de Fuca between Canada and the US one year, and it had a failure. One of its waterstays came off the main hull ... you can see it just below where the aka emerges. The waterstay on that boat is used to form a triangle, which really stiffens up the whole beam structure a lot.

In the next photograph here, we can see that *Magic Hemple's* aka has broken off, right at the main hull. And that little piece of metal my wife is holding there in the foreground is one of those fittings that one puts on the piece of a wire, where it's basically a hook. And it hooks into a specially made hole in a mast and becomes a rigging attachment point.

The advantage is that you can vary the angle that the shroud emerges without having to have any special fitting there. But the hook broke off this thing, and when that happened, the aka itself, just being a slender tube, was not strong enough to hold the load. So it broke off, and the boat capsized in the middle of the race and almost sank.

There was almost loss of life because the water was very, very cold. Fortunately, another race boat came by and picked the sailors up, and they rescued the boat later on too. These photos were taken when I surveyed it afterwards.

During my survey, I found out that the water stay -- the cable that attaches to the main hull and goes up and fastens to the outer end of the aka -- was about 15% under-strength for this boat. It had survived this way for a long time. There probably had been some fatigue from all of its racing past.

The pieces that broke were probably the original equipment. The waterstay eventually broke though. So that tells us when it comes to akas (crossbeams), they need significant safety factors built in. If the akas are comprised of metallic components, those metallic components probably have to be looked at with a definite life, and they need to be changed every once in a while just because of their potential for fatigue failures.

In my opinion, the water stay should not only have been strengthened or increased initially, but it also should have been replaced before this failure occurred. A brand new waterstay of the same size just may have survived. Safe working loads for cable assemblies of that sort are issued. But generally speaking, the manufacturers have some safety factor just for the variation in manufacturing tolerance of these sorts of components. A newer stay would probably have survived the overload. In its aged condition, with a lot of fatigue on it for all that time, it broke.

Signs of Potential Problems...

The next photographed here shows the junction of the forward aka to the main hull of a trimaran. You can see that there have been some problems occurring. I don't know what's inside this boat ... I wasn't able to look inside. But the fact that there's a crack right along that joint, and that there is rust leaking out of it, tells you right away that there are some significant problems here.

This is a wooden boat. But to have rust leaking through like that means that probably the crack goes all the way through that underwing panel, and there's probably something going on inside the boat that nobody has addressed yet. It needs to be addressed, however, if they're ever going to use the boat again.

That particular area of the boat is subject to heavy wave impingements. When the boat is being driven hard to weather on the leeward side of that big bow, waves coming off the main hull will go up and splash that underwing and hit it really hard. We can easily understand that there's probably some deformation in those panels there. The panels are probably deforming slightly inboard, which is what precipitates the crack right in that area. That crack should have had heavy, heavy reinforcement with fiberglass to stop it from occurring.

I recently heard about a cruising trimaran sailing in the Atlantic, and the sailors weren't in extreme storm conditions or anything, but the boat just fell apart when it encountered a heavy sea. The waves were probably in the 3-4 foot range, and the boat just fell apart. They were rescued after drifting on a life raft for a few days. That is how we were able to know what happened to their trimaran.

You can be assured that there was definitely some type of serious structural issues going on that these guys should have addressed long before they ever took that boat out to sea. The boat wasn't a newly-built boat and the structural problem had likely been there for a while.

Those sailors probably didn't know where to look for such problems though. But their story drives home the importance of having a qualified person examine the boat to see if there are any structural deficiencies. Ultimately, your life depends on it.

I've never made a passage offshore without going up the mast first and then looking at all the metal fittings up the mast, the cable assemblies, and the tangs and bolts, and all that sort of stuff. I was just looking for any kind of faults in them. It's always important to just go through the boat and see if there is anything you I haven't noticed before that has changed. It's just prudent to be very familiar with the pieces of machinery that you're expecting to take you to your destination.

There are all sorts of different factors influencing the structural quality of the boat. In wooden boats, of course, it's degradation of the wood. But even in fiberglass boats, it's degradation of the plastic itself. The matrix can soften if it wasn't built correctly, or if it was not designed properly. Fractures can occur in various places. It's very important to realize that plastic boats, fiberglass boats are not immune to the exact same sorts of problems that wooden boats are. There are a lot of boat owners who probably just assume that isn't the case. But it is.

One thing we haven't talked about here is that the worst duty a small multihull will encounter happens on the boat's trailer. I've surveyed a couple of small multihulls -- two identical boats recently, as a matter of fact -- where this was just the case.

Those boats were sitting on their trailers, and in both cases, the rollers on the trailers had pounded through the bottom of the boats. Keep in mind, these were foam core fiberglass sandwich boats ... very high-end, extremely expensive boats. And yet, they were both damaged on the trailer, just from being trailed around over rough streets and that sort of thing.

Their trailer has actually caused more damage than the boats have ever received out in the surf. As a general rule, trailering is actually the worst service you can give a small multihull. If it is a trailerable boat, the worst service it'll ever get is on the trailer.

Sometimes this is because the trailer isn't properly designed to support the boat. Sometimes it's from mistakes.

Let me tell you about a mistake I once made. I had a trailerable 26-foot trimaran at one time. I was ready to launch the boat for a day of sailing and untied it from the trailer. As I was backing down the ramp there were a bunch of mud puddles on the ramp, and I went through them, thinking they were just shallow. But one of them was really deep. The trailer wheel went into it and bounced, and the whole boat bounced on the trailer. When it bounced, it shifted position, and the trailer supports squeezed the hull too hard, in the area adjacent to the bulkhead. The result was that I cracked the planking. Had I had the boat still been tied onto the trailer, it wouldn't have shifted position aft, and that wouldn't have occurred. But I was anticipating my boat was just going to float off really easy, and I would just loop down the ramp like I usually do with no problems.

It was a lesson learned. When I got the boat untied and hit a really deep pothole, it resulted in significant damage to my boat. It's important for owners of trailerable multihulls to be aware of. You've got to be careful when launching your boat. You've got to take care and make sure everything is well supported.

Cracks...

The next photo here shows the cockpit of a large combination cruising-racing trimaran. You can see that the cabin structure extends forward on the right, and there's a smaller cabin in the stern of the boat of that extends off on the left. You can just see the forward end of it there.

This boat has a full-width cockpit, so the cockpit itself sort of interrupts the tubular structure of the boat. When this boat is sailing, it experiences a lot of those twisting platform loads that we talked about in the previous chapter.

Now, as we go to the next picture here, we can see the underside of the side deck on this boat, where those winches were bolted on. The nuts we're see there are the winches where the winches are bolted and some other fittings on deck. But right at the aft end there, and the far end, you can see where those members meet, that next bulkhead back there. There are some cracks there.

Those cracks are never going to just go away because the winches deforming the deck when the boat is being used because those winches are bolted down to the deck. Then the line is wrapped around them some distance off the deck, which puts tremendous load on that line. That load tries to bend the winch, capsize the winch. So there's a bending load on the deck right there trying to deform the deck.

In addition to that load, the boat itself is experiencing twisting loads on it that are tending to change the shape of that upper portion of the cockpit right there. And the area where that member is attached to that next bulkhead wasn't sufficiently reinforced in order to avoid the flexing that goes on in that area. The result was cracking around those fillets shown in the picture. And those fillets, being rather large, should have been big fiberglass reinforced corners. If that had been done then there's a good chance the cracking wouldn't have happened.

The next question one might have about this situation is whether or not the owner of this sailboat can fix the problem so that he or she doesn't have to get a whole new boat. In think there is. One way to fix it might be to have a person go in there with a grinder and grind away the surface coatings in that area in order to get down to something he can bond to and apply a large amount of fiberglass tape on both sides.

The next photo shows the other side of the same joint. You can see it's significant right there where the seatback combing is and the crack is quite visible.

It obviously has no reinforcing in it at this stage, or else we'd see some fiberglass fibers sort of protruding there and pulling away from each other. But if there were fiberglass fibers in there, the cracking would indicate that there just isn't enough of it. That joint could be made strong enough by putting enough fiberglass over that actual corner right there.

I think that would take care of the problem because that area is a secondary structure in the boat. It really doesn't indicate the whole boat is coming apart or anything. But the cracking in that area does let us know there is deformation occurring in those areas, and it really needs to be addressed.

Epoxy is wonderful stuff. You can glue things together, but those glue joints, in some cases, take loads that the boatbuilder didn't anticipate. When that occurs, as in the case here, it's going to take some extra reinforcement in there to hold pieces together and keep them in good shape so the cracks don't reoccur.

Chain Plates...

The next picture here shows one of the primary areas of concern in boats. It's the location where there is attachment of a chain plate.

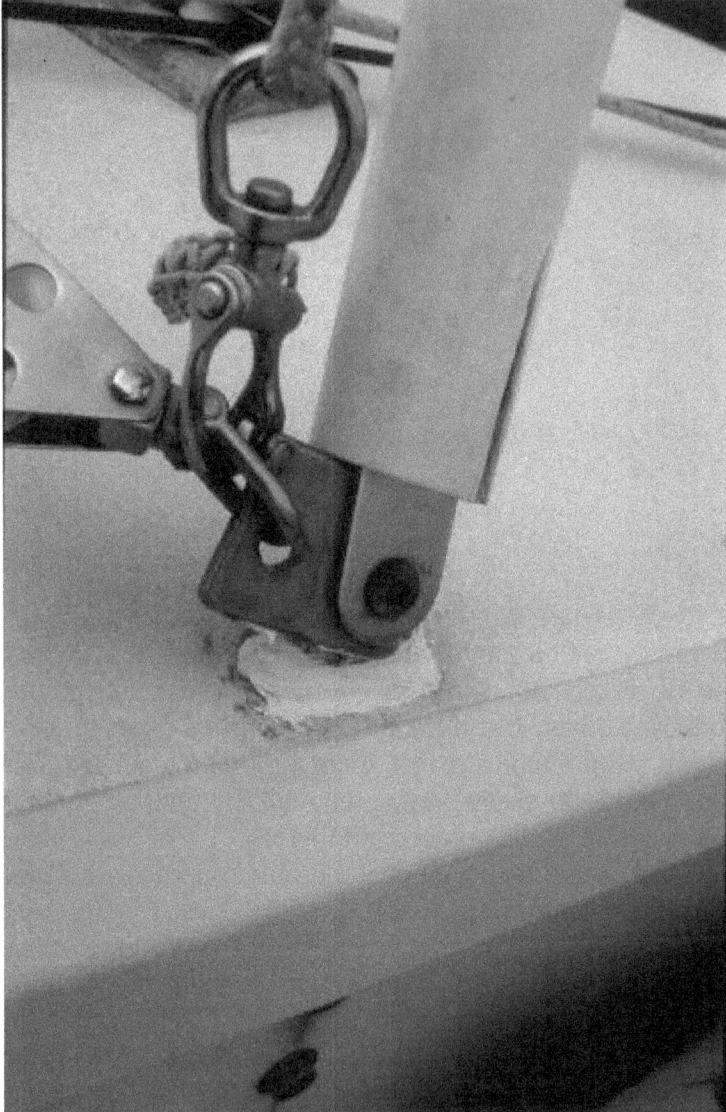

We can see this boat has got some age to it. The chain plate protrudes from the deck. There is a piece of rigging wire attached to it, and there's another tang there, an intermediate tang with a block attached to it. But this is a main structural piece on the boat. The chain plate is almost invisible here because it's on the inside of the boat. And you can see that it's sealed at the deck with a gob of sealant. It looks like the sealant has been applied more than once because it's been leaking.

It's also attached to the side of the boat with a whole bunch of bolts, as you can see in the lower end of the picture. Multihullers should definitely be aware out that chain plates like this do have a definite life, that they don't last forever. They are one of the main points for structural loads in the boat being transferred from a piece of rigging wire to the boat. So chain plates needs to be secured in a fashion that goes beyond any kind of suspicion regarding their strength.

Bolts & Washers...

The last photograph we'll look at in this chapter is of the inside of another boat. Here are bolts coming through the side of the boat that attach the main shroud chain plates to the boat.

There is nothing really wrong with this. The wood you see there isn't the hull side of the boat. It's what is known as a "doubler" piece. In other words, it's another piece of wood that was glued on the inside of the boat. closely fitted in between the stringers, and serves to double up that wood so there was more than an inch of thickness in the wood those bolts are going through. Those bolts are under extremely heavy load. They are half-inch bolts, and this is a 52-foot catamaran.

I personally think one fault here is that the washers used underneath the nuts here -- large fender washers -- deform rather easily. They're not heavy-duty, as they should be. They deform and they're crush the wood right there. What would be better would be to use a larger plate with two holes drilled in it, so the load could be spread out over a much larger area.

That's my only comment here though. This boat is a certified boat. It's been in service for a long time. It's done a lot of service. It has probably been sailed a couple hundred days a year for at least15 years. So it's hard to fault it for not being strong enough. The point here is that there are better ways to transfer the load from the chain plate through those bolts into the side of the hull and make things secure.

This finishes our chapter about structural loads. We've seen there are many places to look on a multihull where there is something bending or resisting a load or taking a load or transferring a load somewhere else.

Halfway through a two-year cruise through the South Pacific with my wife, I remember her being scared a little bit because she knew the shrouds were under an amazing amount of tension during the storm conditions we encountered once in a while. I mean, you could twang the shroud and it would sound like a middle C note.

She started to be aware of the loads and understand the tremendous pressure that was involved. It became rather obvious to her.

Our boat was a Searunner 37 trimaran, which featured a center cockpit. It had a large truck cabin over the main hull, with a huge hole cut into it for the cockpit. The cockpit area is nice and secure. It allows the sailors to be a long way from the water in any direction, and they've got full visibility of the entire boat. But what happens is that the boat bends when sailing it hard. The head stay sags to leeward and pulls on the back stay, and the mast pushes down on the middle of the boat.

A demonstration of what it was doing to the boat occurred one day when we couldn't get the hatch board out of the forward companionway hatch. Those hatch covers reside in a tapered slot. The opening is smaller at the bottom than it is at the top. And it's tapered on the sides just slightly.

Normally, one can simply drop a cover in there, and it's nice and secure. But one day, we were sailing hard to windward and tried to get the hatch cover boards out. They wouldn't budge. It was obvious the boat was changing shape just enough, from the shrouds pulling up and the mast pushing down, so that it was closing up the hatch hole we'd cut for the companionway, just enough to jamb the boards in there. That was a clear demonstration of the stress and strain going on at that moment.

Strain occurred to accommodate the stress, and that strain closed up the hole. That sort of thing happens everywhere on a multihull. If you get out on its platform and jump up and down on one of the hulls, you'll feel the thing vibrate. It shouldn't deform enough to really see it, of course, but you can feel the vibration in your feet. It's a result of all of those bits and pieces bending just slightly and vibrating back to their normal place. They are always flexible to a minor degree.

CHAPTER FOUR
TYPICAL PROBLEM AREAS IN MULTIHULLS

In this chapter we're going to talk about typical problem areas in multihulls that haven't been properly cared for. In other words, we're going to identify things that a multihull owner may encounter if their boat isn't properly cared for. And we'll also discuss subjects that are related to the proper care of multihulls in general.

As a multihull owner, what you have is almost a living, breathing organism. In that sense, we might say that your boat takes care and proper feeding.

As we start off with the first image here, we see the bow of a boat. The focal point here is this cowl ventilator.

Boats, whether they are plastic / fiberglass or wood, all suffer badly from condensation. Condensation is the biggest enemy I can think of for any boat … besides potential corrosion in the water from corrosive sources. I think ventilation causes more damage than anything else.

A multihull owner's goal in dealing with condensation is, in all weather and in all cases, trying to equalize the inside and the outside temperature of the boat so that the water does not condense. The warm air on the inside of the boat that is carrying a lot of moisture doesn't condense on cold surfaces as the daily temperatures swing from day to night. When it does accumulate water on the inside due to condensation, that water finds its way down into the woodwork. It finds its way into the metalwork. It finds its way into the fabrics. It finds its way everywhere and causes nothing but trouble.

I am a big believer in passive ventilation, meaning it's good to use ventilators that just stay open. As long as they're open, you don't have to do a thing. The breeze just blows through the boat, and the temperature is equal. The boat stays dry and doesn't create mildew, and that is good for all of the materials in the boat.

The owner of this multihull has installed other cowl ventilators for other parts of the boat. Some are pointed in one direction and some pointed in another direction, so that they actually form a flow path through the boat.

Also, on the inside of the boat, it would be very important for the owner to have small holes in all of the compartments, leave doors open, that sort of thing, so air can flow through and reduce the potential for condensation.

Basically, if you close a boat up, it can become a solar still. There is a lot of inherent moisture in there to begin with, and all it needs is a real drop in temperature to create cold sides on the boat. All that moisture then comes out of the air and condenses on those surfaces; they become covered in fresh water. And that's what does the damage.

Let me emphasize that this is a problem for plastic fiberglass boat as well as wooden boats. I can't tell you the number of trailerable trimarans made in fiberglass that I've seen with terrible problems on the inside.

The manufacturers of these multihulls typically coat them with a fuzzy stuff that I refer to as "monkey fur." When water condenses in it, it's a perfect generator for creating mildew. When mildew gets into that fabric, it's almost impossible to get rid of it. It just turns dark.

Whenever I survey a boat, I jump into the cockpit, open the hatch and stick my head inside and take a breath. If I can smell mildew then I know I can smell mushrooms. I've discovered mushrooms in boats the size of my fist. I'm not kidding! Such conditions can result simply from lack of ventilation.

Proper Ventilators for Specific Areas...

As we look at the second image here, we can see a multihull that has ventilators on the ama bows, on the right-hand side of the photograph. There is a little cowl ventilator there.

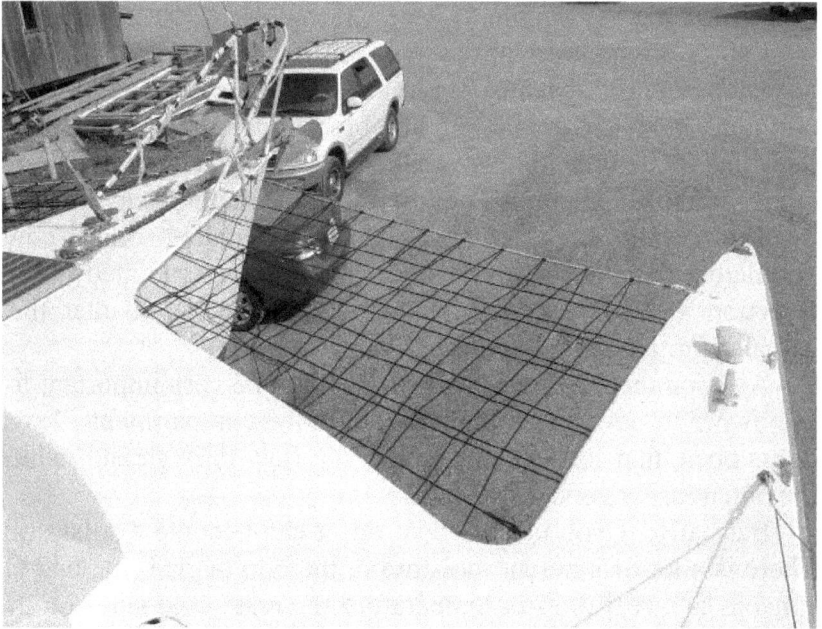

There's another cowl ventilator on the stern. This was my boat, 40 years ago. It is a Searunner 37 I owned called *Bacchanal*. It has cowl ventilators on the foredeck and on the after deck, and they're pointed in opposite directions.

The inside of those ventilator holes stayed perfectly dry and I never had any trouble, even in wet weather. When sailing, of course, those cowl ventilators came off. They just pop right out. They can either stick or slide into the fitting. So when sailing, a sailor will take them out and replace them with deck plates, which mount flush with the deck. Then the boat is ready to take sailing.

Ventilators can accidentally catch lines, so they have to be carefully positioned. One solution would be to put a line on a bridle in order to keep it from snagging on a ventilator. In the photo we just saw, there is a cleat right behind the ventilator that allowed me to lead a line from the chock on the inboard side of the bow, from the anchor bridle, right up to that cleat, in order to just bypass the cowl ventilator. It would wind on counterclockwise.

What I would normally do on my boat is install the ventilators as soon as the boat stops traveling. The goal is always to try and keep the boat dry when it's not sailing. Jim Brown likes to position those cowl ventilators on the hull sides of his boat. He installed his on the inboard sides of the amas of his trimaran, instead of the outboard sides. In so doing, he was able to have them face forward, slanted down just slightly. He did that so when it rains hard, no rain water comes into the boat. This was his approach to achieving the ventilation effect.

If a sailor applies Jim's approach, they just have to remember there is ventilator down on each ama. Before going sailing, the ventilators have to be removed and the covers for those holes have to be installed.

The same idea applies to owners of small multihulls. If their boat has just deck plates in the amas, as a way to access the interior of those amas, then when the boat not in use, the deck plates should be unscrewed and removed. Those access holes should be opened up so the hulls can breathe inside.

If any water did accidentally get in, from rain or something, then just mop it out after it accumulates in the bilge. It's not a big deal, but you wouldn't want the water to just lay in there for a long period of time.

If one has deck hatches of any kind then they should be popped open whenever the boat isn't in use. If they are hinged hatches then just prop them open and create a crack opening. That goes a go a long way to equalizing the inside temperature of the boat with the outside temperature.

It's the temperature that's the problem. Warm air carries moisture; cold air is drier. When there is a temperature changes, all of that moisture can come out of the air and condense on cold services. So you've just got to let temperatures equalize, or get close to being equal, in a hull so nothing happens. Even in a fog, nothing will happen.

The third photograph here shows a whole bunch of things. We have a mushroom ventilator, right on deck, front and center in the picture. Those things are wonderful. They're passive ventilation.

Mushroom ventilators pull air out. You've got to have an air in source if you're going to use those kinds of mushroom ventilators though.

In the case with this boat, there was a back window that you can't see in this photo. This back window was on the very stern end of the boat being shown in the picture there. That back window was almost never latched; it always stayed open. It was a tilt open window Jim Brown designed into the stern castle of the Searunner models he drew up. Those back windows were nice features because a sailor could leave them open, even in the rain, and water wouldn't come into the boat. They provided wonderful ventilation.

This multihull also had a skylight hatch, which is shown over the stern castle. That skylight hatch was normally propped up.

There were also ventilation hatches in the galley of this boat. You can see they've got nonskid strips on them. They were smaller hatches that could be propped open when cooking, or something of that sort. They could be opened for ventilation and, depending on which way the wind was blowing, one could usually leave them open in the rain.

As one may have guessed by now, ventilation is a big deal with me. It makes a multihull so much more comfortable to live in. It keeps your clothes dry, it stops the mildew and stops rot. It's very important.

Ventilation of Deep Interior Areas...

In this next photograph, we see the interior of the typical multihull. These are known as stringers, and they're normally arranged at 90 degrees of the planking. Stringers tend to become carriers of water. Each one of those stringers can generate a nice little river from any condensation that may form on them. And if there's condensation going on, that river is just channeled downward into the next frame. All that water then piles up against the frame and just sits there.

In this boat, we can see the bulkheads have been nicely filleted in with complete fillets. But as is often the case with older boats, before epoxy was commonly usage, any excess water in areas such as this would sink into the interior plywood and grain, thus creating a very difficult situation for the long-term survival of the plywood. In other words, any moisture build-up would promote a rot situation.

Keeping a boat drained, keeping it dry on the inside, is very important. Incidentally, the reason I took this picture was because I inspected this area during a survey of a boat. This was a large, passenger-carrying catamaran. This is an exhaust hose we see running through the structure. And it had a rather long length. There was about 6 feet of it there that was unsupported. It's pretty heavy hose. We can see it's connected to through-hull fitting which is above waterline, so it doesn't require a seacock.

As we can see, it had this little bellows thing that allowed it to self-align when it got there. And that bellows thing, right at the through-hull fitting there, was taking all the vertical load of that piece of hose. It was a thinner piece of rubber, which was eventually going to fail.

The reason I took the picture is to show the need that that exhaust hose really needed to be supported somehow, and it would be very easy to put a piece of wood between the stringers at the top there and just run a tape or band or something around the hose to hold it up and stop it from potentially failing. A failure with that hose would cause all that exhaust to go inside of the hull, which is obviously a bad thing.

Ventilation In The Engine Area...

The next photo here shows an engine. You can see, if you look closely, that it's all rusty. This particular engine compartment was in a 56-foot trimaran. There was no passive ventilation for this compartment at all.

When I first saw the boat, the engine was wringing wet on the inside. This is a perfect demonstration of why one needs passive ventilation. This engine had turned all rusty because it was warm. We have a phrase for this type of situation, *"They ran the boat hard, and they put it away wet!"*

When a multihull owner does that their boat just gets wetter. One of the things I think should happen in engine rooms is they should have good, passive ventilation along with good, powered ventilation -- such as a blower.

When a boat like this comes back to the dock after use, and the engine is cooling off, the owner should be letting a blower run for quite some time after shutting the engine down. That will start the process of exhausting all the hot air that is in there. It'll also pull in some cooler air which will help cool the whole thing down. In the end, there would be much less condensation occurring overall on this machinery.

Proper ventilation is something good boat designers make provision for in the boats they draw up. Boat owners need to have enough ventilation coming in to supply the engine with air and to supply cooling for the compartment itself. Then there has to be enough ventilation to take air out.

For Coast Guard Certified boats, there are rules on how much ventilation area is required for X amount of horsepower. A multihull designer has to meet requirements in the CFRs (Code of Federal Regulations).

For pleasure boats (and the boat in the depicted photo is a pleasure boat), some designers or manufacturers sort of ignore this issue. Or maybe they're not even aware the problem exists until the boat has been operated for several years. And then, all of a sudden, they get a compliant from the boat's owner that their whole engine compartment has turned into a big, rusty mess.

It's just hard to imagine that the designer of a large craft like this may not have given much forethought to the issue of ventilation in the engine area. But it can happen.

This boat was professionally built. It's incumbent upon the builder to address any flaws in design, if there are any. A professional boatbuilder should know what the standard rules are for proper ventilation. The builder knows the engine has to be supplied with fresh air. It needs enough air not only for intake air to the engine, but also for cooling air to the entire compartment. In this case, the need for cooling air had been totally ignored. When the engine was shut down after every use of the boat, the engine room was left shut up pretty tight with very little passive ventilation.

The builder of this boat may have just been ignorant of the need. But there is a lot of expensive equipment on the inside of this engine compartment. It's deteriorating.

Many would be buyers of a big cruising boat such as this, especially one that has been sailed for a while, been out into the ocean a lot, would probably never assume there is a ventilation issue with the boat. But as we've seen here, they'd be wrong.

In fact, a lot of the problems I've seen working as a marine surveyor come right from the factory. In one case I remember, the factory actually changed the design of the air intakes for the engine compartment to avoid seawater splashing in on the engine while the boat was being operated. (They changed the design in later models of the boat). When a lawsuit was brought against them for damage to the engine, which was caused by their poor design of the intake, they tried to fight the lawsuit. The most damning piece of evidence against them was fact that they did change their design of the engine compartment in the newer boats they built.

What was happening on the early boats they'd built was that if a wave top came by the ventilators, much of its water would just ended up on top of the engine. Within just one year of use, the whole engine looked like a rust bucket. The owner of that boat had to have the engine taken out and rebuilt. Some of the appliances around the engine were already starting to rust too.

The next photograph we're going to look at was taken another engine. The engine in this picture is running. As I look at this, I see both good things and bad things going on here.

The access to this engine is underneath the cockpit of the boat, with no access through the cockpit floor. So this was the access that the owner had, and this is the way the engine was installed. The engine was installed without cutting any other accesses other than this one, which was rather amazing. I thought this was a very difficult access.

The good thing we see is front and center. There is a cooling water strainer in there. And there is the seawater intake on the through-hull just inside the opening.

There is good access to that valve, which is often ignored in boats. Many boatbuilders often put that valve somewhere where it's very hard to get to. If anything happens and you start to keep water in there, jumping down in the engine compartment trying to find that valve is virtually impossible. Whereas here, it's front and center.

The next thing is the strainer. You would want to see if there's any encumbrance to the water intake of the engine to make sure that it stays cool when it's running. Those seawater strainers should be regularly maintained and emptied out of all debris that can be picked up so that it just ensures cooling water can get in.

Then, of course, in the back there, we can just see, on the right-hand side, the muffler. The good news is that the muffler connections are reasonably accessible. At least we can see them. Those are vital because any interruption in the airtight integrity of that exhaust system means that the boat is potentially pumping gas, which you don't want to breathe, into the engine compartment.

This is a diesel engine. It doesn't create CO, so one wouldn't worry about carbon monoxide poisoning, as with gas engine. But still, having diesel fumes of any kind inside the boat is pretty obnoxious, especially if it's close to the galley.

Main Structural Areas…

The next photograph here is one we've seen before and when you see things like this you say, *"Oops, we've got a problem here."* There is water coming from somewhere' it's probably coming in from the hatch on deck.

This boat was probably driven very hard at sea. It has inadequate amounts of reinforcement in that joint between the underwing in the main hull on the forward end near the bow, so it can take getting hit by wave tops and things. But when you see this sort of thing on a boat, it requires immediate maintenance.

In this case, the maintenance may have been left too long because there are obviously some corroding fasteners on the inside of the boat, causing those stains. This requires a really good, thorough investigation of the source of those stains. An assessment of the structure on the inside should be performed, and then a full repair on the exterior, and possibly on the interior.

The next photo is also one we've seen previously. This boat is being driven hard at sea; it's under a lot of load. Structural integrity is just absolutely vital for multihulls. They take a lot of banging around at sea, and you certainly don't want to have to endure a dramatic survival situation because of structural failures happening while out to sea.

If one were to take the boat with the crack in its structure out into the ocean then, in theory, one may be inviting a world of trouble into their life. You don't know what condition is inside that area of the boat. Something is obviously wrong because there is rust leaking out. The rust may be coming from a piece of chain that has been lying in a chain lock in there, but the only way to know is to thoroughly examine that area.

If the damage were caused by just a superficial crack that is leaking, then that would require the least amount of repair. But it appears from this picture that that area is inadequately reinforced for the duty it has been performing. Until it's thoroughly investigated, even though it might not be a huge structural thing (it may not be a huge structural problem), one just doesn't know.

The byword for anybody owning a multihull is that if something looks like it's not quite right, it probably isn't. You ought to make sure all parts and pieces of the boat are in top form. Being in denial can be very dangerous.

The boat needs to keep its sailors afloat. If it doesn't then the sailors are in deep trouble.

Older Wood Boat Issues...

The next photograph here is a typical problem with an older boat. Many older boats were built with inferior materials. This is fir plywood we're seeing here. What occurred on the exterior the boat is that the seam along the top had a crack in it. It has fiberglass over that corner between the deck and the hull side there, and when it cracks, you can see the fiberglass fibers pointing through, right next to the crack, and it looks like a zipper. We call these "zipper cracks."

A zipper crack is really important to fix for a couple of different reasons. First of all, it's on a joint between two pieces of wood. So you've got possibly three pieces of wood involved with the crack. You've got the deck, you've got the hull side, and then there is a stringer on the inside they are both attached to. Any internal damage can affect all three, which would be a real problem.

After further investigation, I discovered this particular zipper crack was generated by a small bit of damage on the hull edge that didn't get repaired immediately after the damage took place. Water had seeped in there and started to corrode steel fastenings.

The fastenings were basically galvanized steel nails. The moisture in the wood probably ate up the original zinc coating, which left the steel nails unprotected, and then the steel started to go. We can see from the picture that the moisture had gone even further down and affected some of the nails that were in the stringers below them.

As it turned out, in order for this situation to be repaired, this whole area had to be cut out and removed and then replaced. One thing I will note is that this was a 40-year-old boat. All things considered, the boat wasn't doing too bad overall.

The interior glue used to build the boat was still holding the plywood to the stringers pretty well. There were no problems there. The real thing was that this boat was built before epoxy came into common usage. So this multihull was sheathed with polyester resin and fiberglass. The polyester resin really wasn't adhering that well to wood, as the picture shows. It was peeling off. In addition to that, the polyester resin was permitting a lot of moisture vapor to go through it. It was pretty much a sieve for moisture vapor.

It was holding out the moisture from actual water droplets, but water vapor was still going through the fiberglass. Modern epoxy resins not only have better adhesion to wood, but they virtually seal out any moisture vapor. The moisture vapor transmission rate through an epoxy coating is virtually zero, if there are no pinholes and it. But with the polyester resin shown in our photo, it wasn't the case.

What the owner of this boat needs to do is repair the boat in epoxy. In next photo, we see the problem close-up. We see what the effect of the moisture was in there.

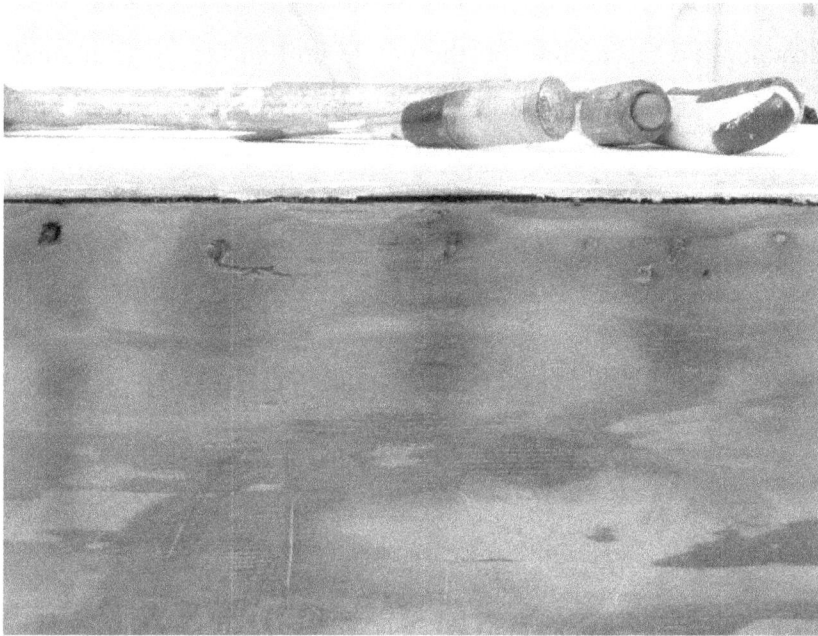

Each one of those nails, in its deterioration, has started to deteriorate the wood immediately surrounding the nail. Actually, these are staples. We can see the staple heads are totally gone. They've started to deteriorate the wood.

It really gets important for these kinds of repairs be taken care of immediately. When a multihull owner sees stuff like this, they've got to repair things. It's not hard to do. If you've got the tools, a problem like this could be fixed in just a few hours. This opening could be opened up and the materials could be prepped for re-lamination. The re-lamination would probably go pretty quickly. Everything would cure, and then there would be a little sanding and then a little painting. You can have the whole thing done, in a few hours, spread over a few days.

In this case an epoxy fix could be applied right over the original coating and protection of the boat. Epoxy sticks really well to polyester resins, which were used in the manufacture of production sailboats and many of the older multihulls built prior to 1980. About 1980, epoxy came into common usage, and most likely anything from '80 forward was built using epoxy.

The next photograph here shows same boat. We're looking at the underwing panel. For some reason, there was some soft wood in the underwing panel. I surveyed it, and I was banging around. I'd tap around on the whole hull surface with a small, plastic-headed hammer and found a soft spot.

Doubler from 20 year old repair

Forward

The picture shows where the soft spot was. We see the bulkhead of the boat there. On the left, at the very bottom, is the hull side, and right, where it says, *"forward,"* is the underwing panel, pretty much going horizontally.

We're looking up at it in the picture. This is one of the main crossbeams going through the boat. We can see that there is a little bit of damage to the wood right on the left-hand side there. You can see some damage to the plywood.

What we did to fix this situation was build up this whole area with another piece of wood and a lot of epoxy. Then we sealed it back up and repaired the underwing panel. The whole repair took less than a couple of days.

The repair wasn't difficult. Repairing stuff like this can be an ugly business because you've got to chip away at the damage and get things back to a point where you can start re-gluing it all back together.

Making a repair like this is fairly simple. You just have to be very brutal with the boat. You may have to take a skill saw and start cutting big holes in it. But once you've got holes with straight edges, it's not hard to glue the whole boat back together again, with the same sort of techniques. You can use butt blocks and plywood, just like it was originally built.

At the moment, we are talking about repairing wooden boats, of course. I do think repairing wooden boats may be a little bit easier for boat owners do themselves, as opposed to plastic, fiberglass boats. A wooden boat seems to involve materials that are more easily understood. Most of the materials are flat; they're not compound curved. Etc.

One problem with fiberglass boats is that they gain strength by having more contours and shapes in the hull. So their manufacturers have a tendency to build them with shapes and contours. And if the boat is cored (we'll see an example in a moment of a cored boat) then the repairs are not simple because you have to replace some of the core material, plus some of the fiberglass. There are right and wrong ways to do it and it may not be knowledge that the owner of the boat has or can easily obtain. That makes doing a repair themselves much more challenging.

Chain Plate Areas...

This photo shows a typical area where I've seen many problems over the years. This is the headstay chainplate for a trimaran.

What happens when you hang a sail on the head stay here is that you get sag. The thing just doesn't stay straight. It doesn't come off the deck at the same angle. The angle changes as the sail is sheeted and the stay is bent back in a big sag. It changes that angle, right at the deck, so the chain plate actually flexes right there on the deck.

As we see in the photo there are two metal pieces, one on each side, so attachments can be done around the head stay chain plate. The chain plate is screwed down to the deck with a bunch of sealant. The sealant has been placed around the chain plate, at deck level, in order to stop water from going down into that low area, where all the bolts are holding the entire chain plate together.

This chain plate will actually work the sealant free, which is something that happens on many boats. It's very, very typical. Water eventually gets in areas like this and the structure underneath gets damaged. It creates a situation where a boat owner is going to have to take out a saw and saw off three feet of the boat, on the bow of the boat, and rebuild it again. This type of situation isn't uncommon either.

All chain plates that emerge through the deck, meaning ones that aren't just bolted on the side of the boat, but emerge through the deck while being connected to the structure below, have to have some sort of a chain plate cover around them so the plate is sealed at the deck. If not, then water can seep below the plate and get underneath it.

The next picture shows another person's solution to this same problem. He just avoided the problem altogether and made that chain plate bolt to the outside of the boat. But in doing so, he didn't fill in the rest of the bow and fare it up.

I suppose this solution, in itself, is good enough if he doesn't mind the way it looks. We could say this is a functional way of taking care of the problem. But one thing he *has* done wrong here though is not got the bend in the chain plate at the same place where the support stops against that face where it's bolted.

In other words, when we look at this chain plate, it just sort of hangs out there in front. So when that chain plate is pulled on, it doesn't want to bend... It wants to bend just below the bend in the chain plate that's already there. That is eventually going to cause the owner of this boat some grief. It's not only going to start damaging the wood that it's bearing against, but it's going to start to bend the chain plate itself and cause some flexing there. The owner could then potentially have some stress corrosion problems in that area too.

We can see in the picture that the position of the toggles show there isn't enough room to slide the plate down because then the toggle pin would impact the deck. So the chain plate is shaped wrong. It should be made longer. The bend should coincide with that shoulder at the very top there. It should extend further above the deck to make sure the toggle and the rigging pin and everything is totally clear of any obstruction with the deck.

I see this sort of thing a lot. Boat owners sometimes put in a chain plate too low. The result is that they end up gouging a hole in the deck in order to get the rigging to fit on it. But then the gouged hole isn't properly repaired, and eventually, leakage gets in there and starts to cause problems.

I don't know of any type of instructional resource that shows sailors how to properly install a chain plate. But they need to be aware that when they get all the components together, all of those components should be dry fitted in order to see where if everything is going to fit together properly.

To just bolt up a chain plate, only to have the rigging pin hole barely above the deck line, is a huge mistake, because once you put the next piece of equipment on to it and find out that it doesn't fit, you've got a difficult repair. Move slowly and make sure everything fits together before moving ahead.

The next picture is the illustration of the problem. Here is a chain plate coming through the deck. It doesn't have a cover on it.

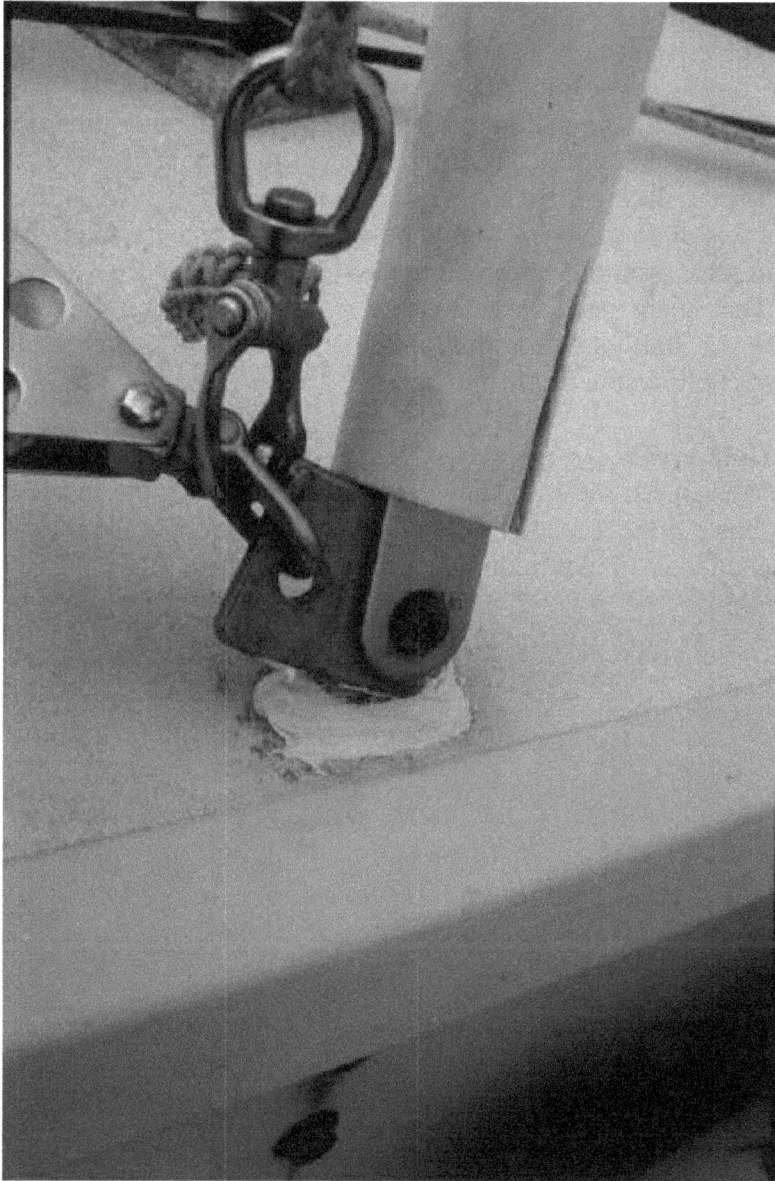

The owner of this boat has obviously experienced some leaks because we can see some fairly new sealant that has been squirted between the deck and where the chain plate emerges. Not only that, we can see an additional tang set in there.

Above it is a turnbuckle. There is a strap toggle on the end of the turnbuckle. We can see another little plate has been slipped in there. This offers a place to fasten the block to, which pulls in another direction.

There is not only a leakage problem there, caused by the fact that there's no chain plate cover, but the leakage is being encouraged by the pulling of the chain plate in another direction, which shouldn't occur. That block ought to be attached to a pad eye on the deck, if that's where the sailor wants it to be located. That sort of arrangement would be designed to take the load. The chain plate should be attached to the rigging wire only.

That chain plate needs to have a pull in just one direction. Once you start using it to pull in the other direction, you'll find it causes nothing but grief.

Bolt Areas...

We've seen the following picture before … it's the inside of the boat, with a bunch of bolts hanging through, which are attached to chain plates on the outside of the boat.

What we're looking at are doublers that were installed to double-up the thickness of the boat to about one inch thick at this point. But those bolts are a half inch long.

This boat is a big catamaran, and has survived quite some time with just the use of fender washers underneath those nuts. But if it were me, I'd have a big plate underneath all those individual pieces of hardware in order to spread the load out over the wood, to prevent the wood from a local failure. We can detect, just barely, that those washers have become disc-shaped and started to crush the wood underneath them. It's not a good situation.

The boat's owner should be proactive about transferring the load more evenly over a larger area. I would definitely recommend a specially made plate to take that load, one with a couple of drilled holes in it … something that's ten times the area of those washers on the inside of the boat.

This next picture here is also one we've seen before. Those bolts in the foreground, at the very, very top of the picture, are attaching great big winches, which are on top of this thing.

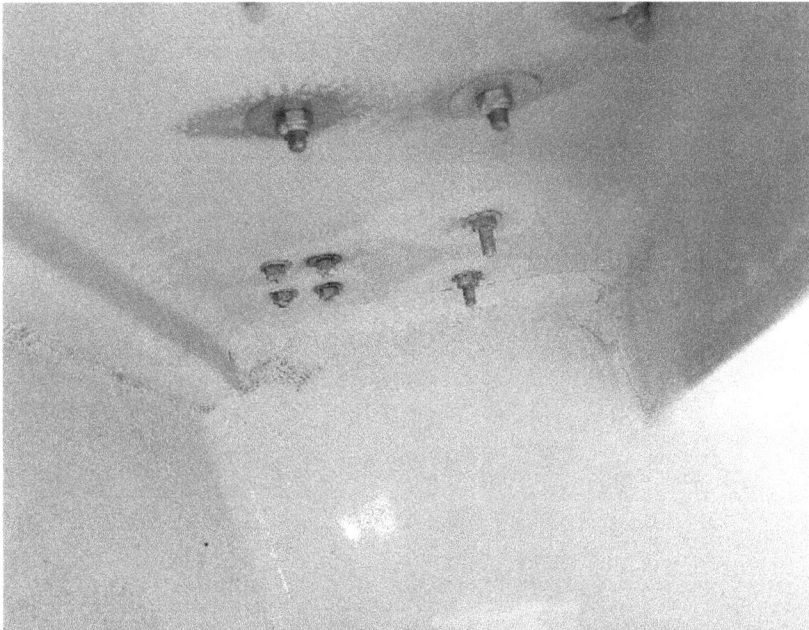

Those winches really ought to have a full-sized disc of metal underneath them. They should have substantial metal underneath them, with a matching hole pattern drilled in it, in order to transfer the load to that entire chunk of deck, rather than just having it locally placed, as it is in the photo. Eventually, those washers are going to deform even more. The material is going to crush and repairs will have to be made because water will seep in there. The end result will be problems in the boat's deck structure.

One thing to consider is that this particular multihull was professionally built. It wasn't just slapped together by some guys in a backyard somewhere. Remember in a previous chapter, we discussed the cracks that are in the background back there, where that surface at the top meets that bulkhead in the back. We noted the whole area lacked proper reinforcement. But then, when it came time to outfit this boat, the builders again took shortcuts and didn't adequately support some of the accessories that they had bolted on deck. So this too was a fault of those "professional boatbuilders."

Biggest Threat to Trailerable Multihulls...

The next image once again shows us a familiar, trailerable trimaran. And we are reminded, once again, that I always tell people that that hardest service a boat like this will ever receive is on its trailer.

And let's go look underneath the trailer and take a look at where the boat is being supported on the trailer. In the photo, we see those black rollers underneath the boat. We can also actually see the boat's bottom is now somewhat deformed. It seems to be sort of caving in.

A number of other boats, from this same manufacturer, have different trailers than this. I don't know why this one had a trailer that permitted the boat's weight to be supported by just those rollers. Other boats had long planks, covered with carpet and so forth, that supported the boats' bottom over a long length. That is a much better way of supporting the bottom of a boat such as this, as opposed to what we see in this picture.

In the next picture, we take a look inside of this boat. This is the very bottom of the boat hull. We can see how it's bulged upwards.

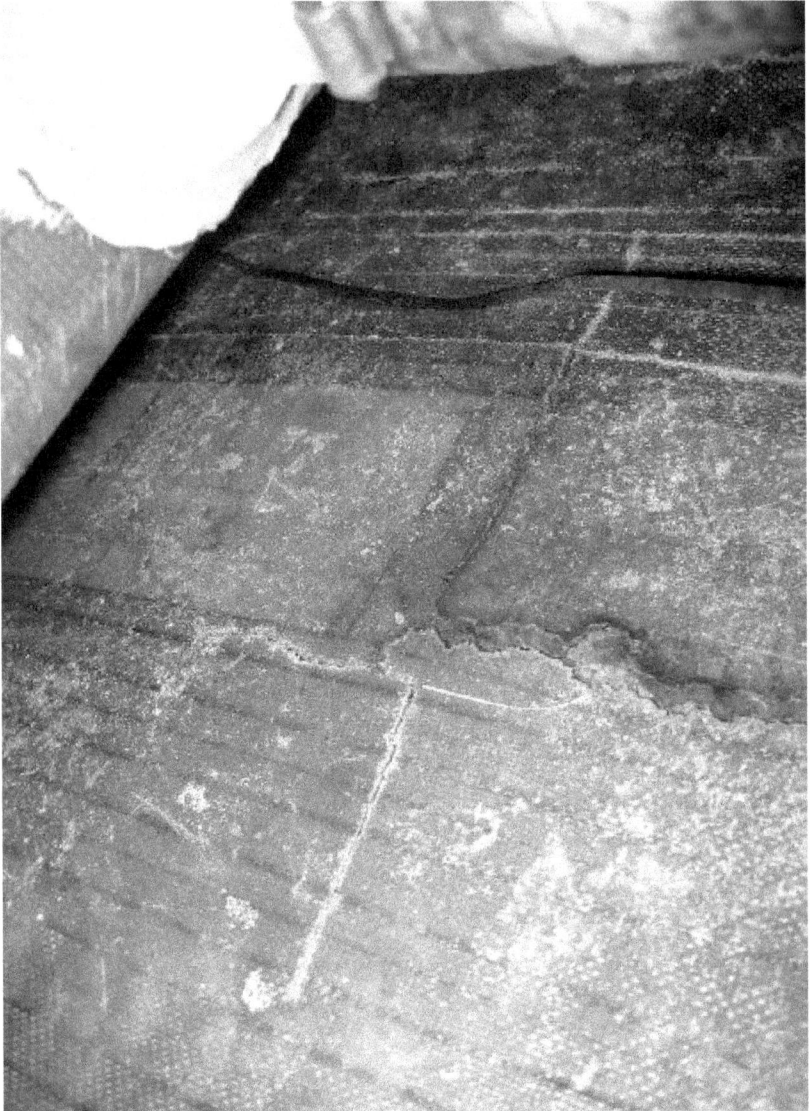

The boat's owner actually anticipated the position of those rollers. He or she put in what looks like a dense coring in the laminate here -- that's the pink stuff we see in the picture. I am guessing that it is a higher-density coring than the brown stuff on the lower side of the picture. But we can see that the fiberglass inner surface of this fiberglass sandwich boat has failed. It cracked.

The rollers underneath the boat are now pushing their way up through the boat. It's not likely that the owner of this boat ever realized this damage was happening because I don't think the watertight integrity of the boat had been breached. I don't think the cracks went through the outside surface of the boat here, meaning the outside laminate of fiberglass. If it had, there would be water in the boat, and the boat's owner probably would have noticed it.

I may be wrong but the white powder we see there may be salt from dried seawater, I don't know. It's hard to tell. But still, if you've got a trailerable boat, and it's on the trailer, the trailer is the most difficult service that the boat will ever see. Be sure, if you've got a trailerable multihull, that it is well supported, so the hull doesn't get damaged.

This sort of damage isn't something that most boat owners would expect to see on a boat like this, especially a well-known production model like this one. And this boat isn't very old either. So damage like this just isn't something most people would expect to see. In light of that, one needs to go the extra mile to make sure their boat trailer is an absolute perfect fit for their boat.

Small multihulls are damaged more frequently on a trailer than when they're in the water. The water is a fairly soft medium. Apart from hitting a dock, there isn't as much opportunity to damage the boat when it' in the water. The boat's trailer, however, is supporting the entire weight of the boat, over just a few points and a small amount of the hull surface.

The actual points of support need to be well-tailored to the boat in order to prevent the trailer from deforming the hull. The boat's hulls are not designed for point loads. They're designed for global, hydrostatic loads that push in evenly over the entire surface of the boat. And so, the types of loads a small multihull experiences on a trailer are very, very different ... and the result can be very damaging.

I once surveyed two trailerable trimarans on the same day, and they both had this same problem. They were both production manufactured boats and, as it turned out, only a few hull numbers apart. Both of them came from different geographic locations in the country, where they were originally sailed, to this one point. And it was amazing to see the identical failures in the boat.

In my opinion, their trailer was poorly designed. It seemed to me that, at one point, this trailer model had some side supports that would have held up the hull sides in order to take a lot of the weight off those rollers. But I think, as these trailers grew older, those supports sagged away from the boat. The result was that more and more of the boat's weight ended up falling on the rollers. And those rollers were not readjusted to accommodate the condition of the trailer in relation to the boat's hulls, which needed much more support than what was supplied by just those rollers.

Those trailerable trimarans ended up slowly sagging downward, further and further, with more of their weight on those rollers. The result is what we see in the previous photo.

Lots of Things To Be Aware Of...

The next photo here are also ones we've seen before. We see a guy sleeping in the cockpit. But we can see that this boat, when it's sailing, has got a whole bunch of different bits and pieces all under loads.

We can see a winch in the picture that's under load. We can see a block, with a line through it, which is attached to a plate somewhere. We can see another block and a bunch of lines. There are deck hatches there that need really secure hold-downs and hinges to hold the hatch closed. If you ever have a hatch come open at sea, or have ever lost a hatch cover at sea because of rotten fastenings or rotted wood, it can be devastating to the safety of the boat. Losing a hatch cover would be a real breach of the watertight integrity; it could result in putting the sailors in very difficult straits. The loss of a hatch would require something to be done before the sailors can safely proceed on their journey.

All of these maintenance issues we're talking about are part of making sure your multihull is fit for its service, which is absolutely paramount. As boat owners and sailors, we can get pretty blasé sometimes about jumping on a boat and going for a sail across the bay. It's not too discouraging to have something break possibly and jury *rig* it and keep on sailing. But if you're crossing an ocean, it's a different story. That is more akin to being something breaking when you're flying in an airplane, up in the air. You just don't have a chance to stop and fix it.

If a cruising multihull suffers from a failure in the middle of the night, in a storm, then it's potentially a serious situation. This makes it incumbent upon sailors to make sure all the things we're talking about here are in good shape.

Electrical Issues...

The next photograph features a rudder. This rudder happens to have some stainless steel underneath the water, which comprises a pivot pin in the lower end of the blade, where it meets the skeg.

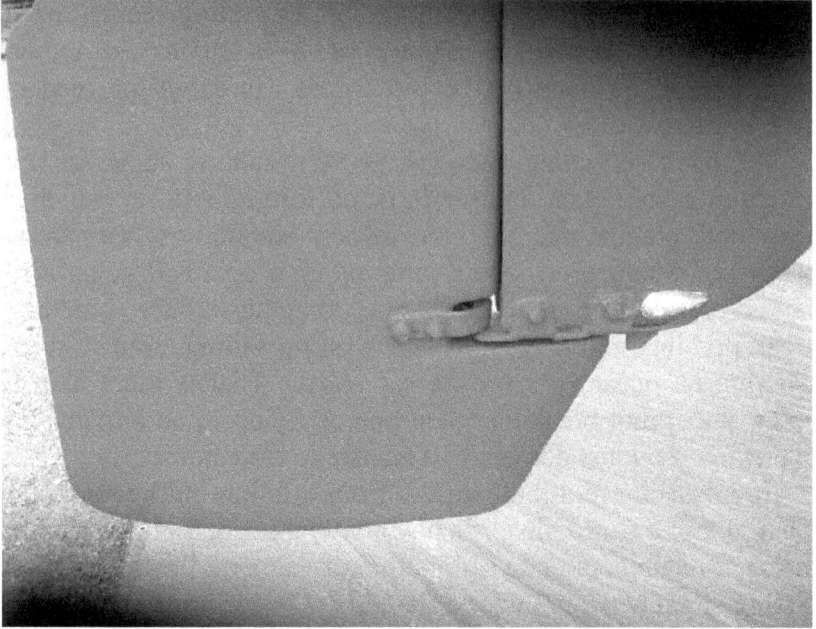

There are a whole bunch of things going on there. But the primary reason for me showing this picture is that there is a zinc anode screwed to the side of the skeg. What we don't see is that there is a little wire pigtail that goes out, and goes underneath one of those nuts that are holding the first fitting onto the skeg. That fitting there is painted over, but it is stainless steel. It's really subject to corrosive forces underneath the water line. So what I want to emphasize is that it's absolutely important for every piece of metal that touches seawater to have an anode attached to it so that it doesn't corrode.

The anodes themselves do corrode. They corrode to save the pieces of metal they're attached to. This means they have to be replaced on a regular basis. That periodic basis is determined by the corrosive forces acting on the boat.

If a boat is at anchor then it may be that those anodes will last a couple of years before the boat's owner has to replace them. If a boat is in the harbor then my guess is it'll be consumed before one year is out. In some cases, it may be consumed before a month is out, depending on where the boat is.

Regular inspection and maintenance must be done in order to check on what the rates of corrosion are in areas such as this. One of the most alarming areas a sailor can ever moor their boat in is right next to a huge steel bulkhead. If a sailor puts their boat into the harbor, and the harbor has actually been dug out of a marshland, or something like that, and one of these big corrugated steel bulkheads has been installed in the harbor with a dock next to it, then it's a potentially bad area to tie a boat nearby.

If a sailor ties their boat up to that kind of a dock, its steel bulkhead will have an incredible corrosive force. It will want to pull ions from any kind of metal off a boat. It requires a lot of zinc to withstand that kind of attack.

Another source for a potential problem is defective wiring onboard other boats that are plugged into shore power. They may actually be putting electricity out into the water, which is not only dangerous from a health standpoint, if someone falls into the water, but it's also very, very damaging to all underwater metal.

I could tell you plenty of horror stories on this topic. One in particular that I remember is when a sailor bought a brand new boat, tied it up to a dock and then returned soon afterwards in order to go sailing. He discovered the engine battery was dead. So he went to see a friend who owned a gas station and borrowed one of those big gas station battery chargers -- the ones on wheels. Then he heeled it down to the dock, plugged it in, clamped it on his battery and then went off to have lunch, figuring the thing would be charged up by the time he came back from lunch. What he didn't realize, however, was that he had accidentally hooked it up backwards. He hooked the positive terminal to the negative and the negative to the positive, so the battery charger was actually pumping 12 volts plus down into the grounding system into the boat. His particular boat didn't have a charger, an inverter or anything like that. It had the AC ground hooked right to the DC ground. What he was doing by accident was pumping 12 volts DC, at about 100 amps plus, into the water. My boat was 60 feet away, not connected to shore power or anything, and my propeller turned black. Another boat, 30 feet away, on the same dock, also had common AC/DC ground. That boat had two, 30-inch propellers de-zincified, meaning that it was taxed so badly by that situation, the zinc left the propellers entirely, leaving almost nothing but pure copper. The boat's owner could just break the tips off of those propellers like a chocolate bar.

As that story shows, damage can occur very quickly during a situation like that. I heard of one where a fault occurred where the AC onboard shore power main line got frayed and then contacted the boat ground. There were children in the water swimming nearby. One child was so badly incapacitated by the electricity in the water that the child drowned. When officials examined that tragedy, they found they could test the water actually get a reading on the electricity that was in the water up to 60 feet away.

It happened to be lethal within about 15 feet of the boat. Anybody swimming within 15 feet could be totally incapacitated and drown. That is obviously a worst case situation for what we're talking about here. But it does serve to illustrate the dangers involved with these sorts of issues.

On Wiring...

Rules for new boat manufacturers are that they install an ELCI, which means "electrical leak circuit interrupter." An ELCI would shut off all of the electric connections in the boat in order to keep this sort of tragedy from happening. It's another piece of equipment that should now be installed on all multihull cruisers nowadays. It's not really all that expensive, but it can save people's lives.

As a matter of fact, standard ground fault circuit interrupters (GFCI), which are now required for household circuits in the kitchen and so forth, are also required for boats in galleys and in the engine room and in the toilet area, head compartments.

While we're talking about wiring, let's go to the next image here. I hate to tell you that this boat is a certified vessel. It was certified by the Coast Guard. We have here what is rather typical in old-boat wiring. It's sort of a rat's nest.

Those wires should be organized; they should be bundled up. They also should be supported every 18 inches or less. The DC wires should probably be separate from the AC wires. And one of the things here that this boat owner got fined for is that the battery on the right is an 8D. It has a tremendous amount of power. I mean, you could weld metal together with it because it's got that kind of storage power. What is required now is that main red wire coming out of the battery needs to have a fusible link or a fuse in it. It's one of those big fuses that are the size of a cigar.

You can see fuses like this in houses and so forth. But nevertheless, if there was any kind of a short fault with any of those wires coming out of that, there's enough power in that battery to start an instant fire and burn the boat down. A fusible link is an attempt to prevent that from happening.

This particular boat is 52 feet long. A boat this size has a sizable diesel engine. This battery serves not only as an engine start but also the house power system. It's not an outsized battery for this boat. But the wiring issue is something the owner, regardless of whether or not the craft was professionally built, should have paid a lot more attention to.

Normally, a boat designer doesn't even provide builders with an electrical system for the boat because that entirely depends on what sort of appliances the owner wants to put on the boat. But the boat should be wired to guidelines provided by the American Boat and Yacht Council (*ABYC*). Their standard is the standard that I have to survey boats to meet.

The wiring standards are fairly simple and straightforward. If wiring systems get complex then rules can get more complex. But for a simple system on a boat the rules tend to be very simple.

About Fiberglass Hulls...

The next photograph here shows a typical keel boat bottom. You may now be thinking, *"What does this have to do with multihulls?"* Well, multihulls are built out of the same materials as other boats. And I just didn't happen to have a photograph of the multihull with zits on the bottom. So that is what we're going to look at here ... those little bumps on the surface of the boat's bottom there.

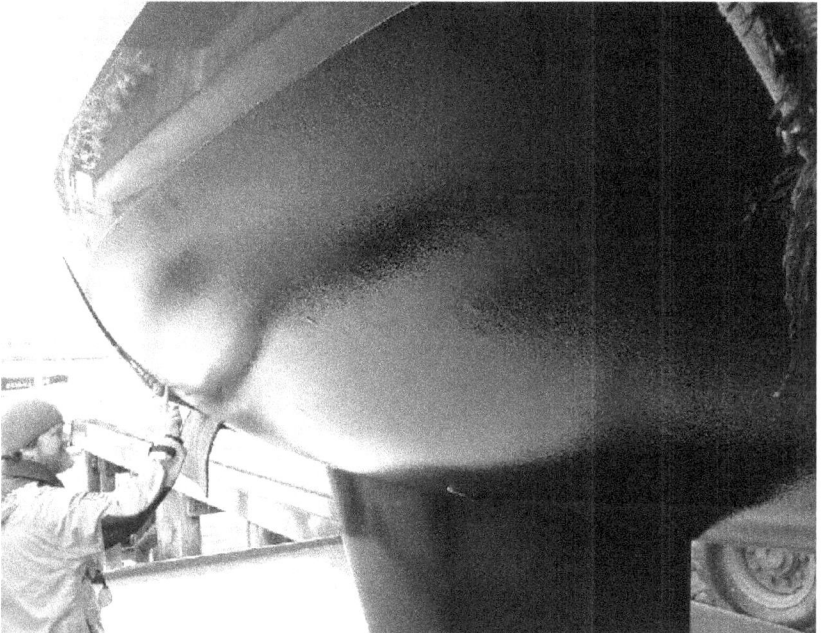

That condition is what is known as "osmotic blistering." On this boat, the blisters were not large. They were about the size of a quarter. Maybe one or two were the size of a half dollar. These blisters are basically caused by the failure of polyester resin to adequately provide a surface service on the boat's bottom.

In other words, the polyester resin used in this application was never designed to be used here. It was really not the right resin to use for boats. But hundreds of thousands of boats have been built with this resin because it was thought to be the most wonderful stuff in the world at the time.

To be more precise, most boatbuilders were using *"isophthalic polyester."* It was actually pretty good resin and didn't result in this type of blistering problem, if used properly. But around 1980, chemical companies developed a new type of polyester called *"orthophthalic polyester"* resin. They sold it to boat companies as being significantly less expensive.

Many boatbuilders, of course, though that was great. So they bought this new resin, and pretty soon they started seeing this osmotic blistering problem. They discovered this new resin was more prone to having blistering problems than the isophthalic polyester had been.

All of these blisters emanate from bubble areas. When you understand how fiberglass boats are built, it makes perfect sense. They have a mold, and the inside of the mold is nice and shiny. (It's what produces the nice shiny surface on the outside of a fiberglass boat.)

The first thing that is sprayed in the mold is a gel coat, which is the paint-like finish on the outside of the boat. That gets sprayed in first. Then, on top of that, they put fiberglass of various types, all wet out with this polyester resin in what they call the matrix.

The first matrix to go into the hull is usually a very light layer of what they call "mat," which is chopped up strands, anywhere from a half an inch to a couple of inches long, laid out all higgely-piggely, in a flat surface. It looks like a piece of really thin felt, with fibers going in all directions. It's non-directional fiber and it goes into the mold and it gets wet out.

The next thing that goes on top of it is usually a heavy piece of cloth, called "woven roving." Rovings are a collection of fibers. In most cases, for the type of cloth that they're using, the collection might be an eighth of an inch wide. It's woven into a cloth that's fairly loosely woven, and when it's packed down, all those fibers sort of spread out. They use a plain weave, so each strand of yarns goes over one and under the next one in order to create an over-under weave. And every time there is a joint

111

where the two fibers cross each other, there is a little hollow space left in there because the cloth is not absolutely flat.

If you look at a piece of canvass or something, and can see sort of a lumpy surface in there, then the same sort of thing is occurring as what we see in our photograph. Everywhere there is a little dip, a bubble will form when they put this all down.

The boatbuilders have rollers that look like a whole bunch of washers, all stacked up together, with little spacers in between. They're called "bubble-buster" rollers, and they're supposed to roll out all of these lumps and press the bubbles out of it so that all those bubble sites fill up with resin. The goal is to end up with no bubbles. So the whole layup consists of fiberglass and matrix. It's hard to do on a compound surface, and it's hard to do over a large surface while working quickly. The fiberglass boatbuilders are laminating many layers of this stuff up, while working at a fast pace.

If they work too fast then a lot of those bubbles will go un-popped. If that happens, then the final product will end up having a whole bunch of these little bubble sites. If we were able to get a close-up shot of our picture then we'd see some of the bubbles are sort of in a line, where all those blisters sort of line up. I've seen entire boat bottoms where the whole thing looked like a crosshatch of lines of bubbles. I could draw a line through one line of bubbles, and another, and then another. What you'd have after doing that would look like a piece of graph paper.

When the bubbles are small like this, it means they're in the first laminate, right next to the exterior surface. And that means they're really not dangerous. In other words, it means they haven't caused any real structural problems for the boat. What is occurring is that water has migrated into that bubble site and combined with some chemistry left over in the matrix that didn't get tied up in the polymer chain; it results in an expanded, larger molecule. When enough of those things get together, they cause a blister.

This type of problem usually occurs on the outside laminate of the boat. These blisters may eventually crack the gel coat. For minor blisters, the repair is as simple as gouging out the blister, then cleaning it out, then puttying it up and painting the entire surface area again.

The real problem is if these blisters are bigger. I've seen blisters up to three or four inches in diameter … and sometimes larger than that. Those go deep down inside the laminate. That situation requires a major repair because the structure is actually prying apart. This is laminated fiberglass, and those larger blisters destroying the inherent strength in that is supposed reside within the solid laminate structure.

Many owners of fiberglass boats don't realize it, but in these types of boats, you can have what appears to be damage in just one specific area, but the real damage is actually running a long way down from that point.

This is particularly true of cored boats, which have a fiberglass skin on the outside, and then coring material with another layer of fiberglass skin on the inside. That is what is often referred to as "*the sandwich.*" This sandwich can be made of foam, or even wood. It can be made of other materials too. But oftentimes, boatbuilders will make the sandwich crisscross, so it can be pushed into a compound curve shape. And those little curves can actually form little open spots, where water can migrate from one area to another. It can create a situation where if the boat owner ever damages the boat in one place, the damage can transfer way down along the way to somewhere else.

I've seen pictures of surveyors who have drilled exploratory holes in the bottom of the boat, because of some damage above it, and water is just pissing out of a hole that they drilled that is a significant distance away from the damage that they were originally investigating. The water is just transferring from the known problem area and revealing that the damage actually extends far beyond that one area.

I personally dislike "sandwich boat construction" because of this problem. They're not only difficult to assess, from a restoration perspective, when damage does occur, but the real difficulty lies in figuring out how far the damage goes until it stops. How far has the damage gone through the laminate? I mean, obviously, you're going to have to pull one skin of the laminate off, and possibly a lot of the coring out, and then replace it again, in order to fix a problem like that. But the initial difficultly is trying to figure out how far the damage goes in the first place.

With fiberglass boats, one may not be able to just easily see where a boat is damaged. A friend of mine bought an old SeaCat, 25, which is a 25-foot, daysailing catamaran. It's a really fast boat. He got it for really cheap. He knew it was in bad shape, but had me come down to take a look at it. I knocked on the side of it and that side seemed sort of flimsy. After pushing a little harder on it, we heard the foam go, *"Crunch, crunch, crunch."* There were areas of this boat where the outside skin was in perfect shape, but the foam inside was rattling around in there all by itself, and the skin on the other side of the boat wasn't attached to anything. The hulls were a mess.

That's what can happen. That's very scary. That's the primary way that a Hobie Cat falls apart. It's what causes their demise.

The older Hobie Cats are foam-core boats. They can get soft and mushy and rubbery if the foam disintegrates or becomes unstuck from it outer skins.

Scampering Up the Mast...

This next photograph here shows me when I was about 25 years old. The reason I've included this image here is so you can see that the mast on this particular boat is totally clean. It wasn't long afterwards that I put steps up that mast.

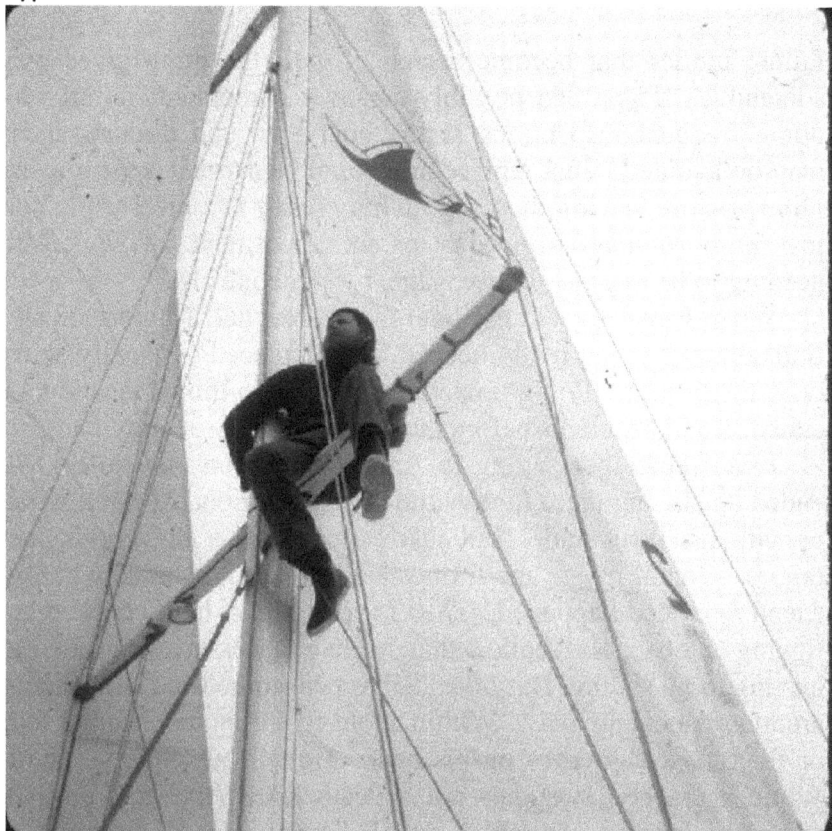

The reason I put mast steps on the mast is because I was making offshore passages in this boat and a sailor really needs to be able to go up the mast in certain instances. If they really need to do it when out to sea then mast steps make the exercise a lot easier. Your very existence out at sea depends on the structural integrity of the boat, including of all those bits and pieces on that mast, which holds up the sails and so forth.

Before every sailing trip, before making any sort of a crossing -- even if it was across the bay -- I'd usually scamper up the mast. After putting steps on it, the climb only took a few minutes. It was my practice to look at everything, see if there's anything had changed, try and see if anything had been damaged or bent or if anything was coming apart. I was always on the look for things that didn't appear to be right. The goal was ascertain, to the best of my ability, that there was a probably of nothing breaking during the trip.

As multihull owners and sailors, we must be vigilant and understand that these boats do run down. They seem to have failure modes that become secret ... until the thing gives way somehow. If you can possibly discover component failures by doing frequent inspections of the boat then bad circumstances may be avoided. Just replace any components that appear to be failing before leaving the dock. It may result in a nicer trip. You just might yourself from a lot of embarrassment (or worse) by needing to be rescued, mid-voyage, by someone else.

When I investigated my boat in this manner, I'd periodically find something that really needed to be replaced -- usually about once every year. Being proactive about these things let me take care of small problems before they became big problems.

I can remember sailing to American Samoa one time. We ended up staying there for a while. Another friend of mine sailed in with his boat, and I had just experienced a big component failure. One of my swage fittings had cracked. I shared with my friend what had happened. Then I asked him if he'd checked his rigging lately. He replied that he had checked things before leaving to go sailing. But I decided to take some time and wander around his boat anyway. Within about five minutes, I found four or five cracked swages on his boat. He was absolutely aghast. While a cracked swage is not a death knell (the crack has to proceed a long way before it really compromises its strength), it does mean the clock is ticking. That piece of equipment is going to die eventually. It had already started the process and had to be replaced.

We mutihullers need to be ever vigilant for broken stuff. I've broken plenty of stuff. I broke stuff on the first weekend I was out with my boat. I once broke some special blocks that I'd designed for the running back stays, to keep them really down low to the deck. We were headed across San Francisco Bay in the trimaran, going lickety-split, under full sail, having a great time, and all of sudden, "*Ka-boom!*" It sounded like a shotgun blast going off. One of those blocks just totally disintegrated. I was lucky I didn't lose the mast. There was enough redundancy in the rigging on the mast that I didn't lose it. But I went back there and I looked and I thought, "*Oh wow ... that thing takes a lot more load than I thought it did.*" It was a real surprise to me. I ended up rebuilding those blocks out of much heavier material and then bolted them in. They lasted for a long time afterwards.

This last photograph here is a favorite of Jim Brown's. What it really depicts for us, however, are those steps on the mast.

The only reason he got this photograph is that he walked up the mast while he was being visited by all these Kuna Indians, in the San Blas Islands, while sailing down in the Caribbean. They had all come up to the boat in order to sell textiles.

Jim was able to scamper up his mast using the mast steps and get this fantastic picture. So I guess that is another reason to put mast steps on your mast ... you may get to take a great picture at the top of the mast.

CHAPTER FIVE
TYPCIAL COMPONENT FAILURES ON MULTIHULLS

In this chapter, we're going to talk about typical component failures found on multihulls. What we're going to talk mostly about, however, centers on the rigging of these boats.

There are plenty of different component failures that occur on boats. Lots of them are common to all boats. There are things that happen with engines, exhaust elbows and the electrical system. Those are regarded as more common failures.

Rigging involves components that most people really don't understand very well. There's a lot to look at and there are ways to prevent things breaking in order to avoid both danger and embarrassment.

Wrong Solutions for Common Situations...

We can start with the first photograph here. This is a chain plate from my old Searunner 37 trimaran, which had about 40,000 miles on it by the time this plate was removed. This chain plate shows an elongated hole where the head stay was attached.

We can see on the upper edge of the hole that it's sort of egg-shaped or oval-shaped. It's been flanged over and this chain plate did need replacement. It was replaced with heavier stock to prevent that elongation from occurring again. I'm actually amazed that, at some point, it did not break.

The load this chain plate was under actually deformed the metal. That should never occur to any great degree. If anybody sees something like this on their boat, especially where there are pin terminations for rigging wire, and that sort of thing, then the chain plate should be replaced immediately.

The next image is obviously identifying the position of this particular chain plate. This is a sister ship. And we can see the chain plate emerging through the deck.

There is some fairing on the hull, just forward of that chain plate, which is very typical for Searunner trimarans. We've seen this picture before, in a previous chapter. But what's important here is that, on Searunner trimarans at least, the sail is not tacked down to the deck. When we sheet the sail in, the pull along the foot of the sail is not terminating at the deck. It actually terminates about a foot and a half above the deck. The sail pulls back on the head stay.

As a result, the angle that the head stay usually makes with the deck changes. And when that changes, it actually tries to bend the chain plate ever so slightly. In time, over years sailing, this bending of that chain plate back and forth will tend to harden up the chain plate and create stress fatigue. We've actually had these chain plates break in Searunners. The breakage was partially a fault of the way the chain plate was bent because it has to have an angle bend it, as we saw in the first picture. If the chain plate is bent at a very sharp angle, then that sharp angle represents a stress riser that tends to make the thing fail.

But motion of bending back and forth is the thing that causes failure on most chain plates. They're really designed to take load in only one direction, and they're only happy doing so. Chain plates don't like bearing loads in more than one direction.

In this photograph, we see a fellow who obviously had the same boat, with the same head stay chain plate. He just omitted the fairing that is in front of the boat, in front of the chain plate.

It appears that he just cut it off and decided he wasn't going to go through that again. Well, the fault with what he's done here, if we look closely, is that the chain plate is bent so that the top end of the chain plate is probably going to be at about the same angle as the head stay. But that bend is well above the part of the boat that supports the chain plate.

If the chain plate is going to be bent back there then we can imagine as a load is applied to that chain plate, it's going to want to bend in another place right there. The point here is that chain plate should have been located lower down so that its bend would coincide with the support that the hull gives it. If you give a chain plate a chance to bend, it's going to exhibit this fatigue-type problem and it will eventually fail.

It appears as if he just put the chain plate on the boat to the degree that the fairing had been cut back and then didn't cut the chain plate correspondingly so that it fit right. He should have cut that notch down a little bit lower in order to get the chain plate to fit up against the deck.

By doing that, of course, he would still have a problem because the pin would then need some clearance so that the sailor could get to the pin and put a cotter key on it, on the other side, which would have interfered with the support he had arranged there. If you're ever trying to make these sorts of modifications on your boat, just be sure that the chain plate is going to fit in place, as you go along, before the actual installation.

New Component Failures...

In the next photo here, we see the head stay chain plate from my old trimaran, *Bacchanal*. We were in the South Pacific at the time, in Fiji, next to that island seen on the chart.

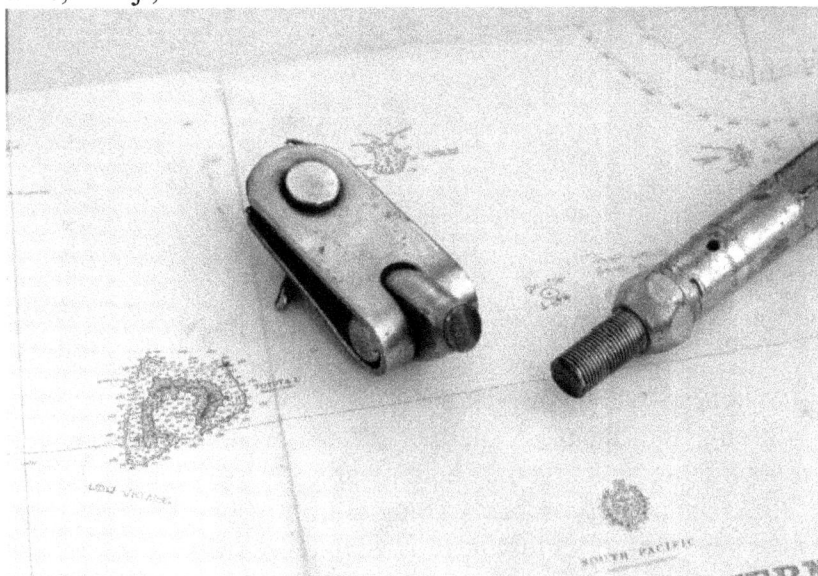

This was the biggest turnbuckle in the entire boat. It snapped right where the head of the eye is on the bottom of that threaded connector, in the turnbuckle. I still don't have a good idea why that occurred because there was total freedom of that toggle. It wasn't being restrained to the point where it was tending to bend the turnbuckle.

What I do think may have happened was that the chain plate was stainless steel, the pin was stainless steel, the toggle was stainless steel, and all of those things there that are supposed to have freedom of motion. But stainless, when it rubs against itself, tends to gall. It's sort of a soft metal, and it has this nasty tendency to sort of try and weld itself together when you're turning one piece of stainless against another under high load. And it may be that this galling tendency, sort of trying to weld itself together under load sort of thing, was restraining the toggle motion -- the pin hinge motion -- of the thing and caused the turnbuckle to bend, which fatigued it enough to the point where it finally broke.

It's unlikely that a visual inspection of this component would have prevented this failure. I may have seen a hairline crack starting on this thing, before it broke. But it would have been very, very difficult to see because the failure occurred right at the base of the threads. The location it broke was right where the threaded portion of that terminal stops.

This was a very nicely made turnbuckle. The threads were rolled, which is much stronger than if they had been cut by a machinist. The body of the turnbuckle was chrome-plated bronze. The threads were stainless steel, of course, so there were dissimilar metals there, which were quite happy to work with each other. It was one of the highest quality turnbuckles on the market ... or so I thought. I put my faith in it. It was 5/8 in size, the biggest one on the entire boat. All the rest of them were all 1/2 inch. I'd used this 5/8 size because I didn't want to compromise the head stay. And yet, for some unknown reason, it still broke.

At the point that this turnbuckle broke, our trimaran had sailed just under 20,000 miles. Since then, this boat has probably sailed the same number of miles using the turnbuckle that replaced the broken one we're talking about here. It is a possibility that the failure was caused by a manufacturing defect, but I doubt that. As I've already said, I still don't have a good idea what the actual cause of this failure was.

We have to look at this next picture fairly closely. This is the aftermath of the turnbuckle failure on my boat. As we can see, the turnbuckle has been removed. The head stay now terminates in two lanyards of 1/4" flexible wire that I happened to have onboard.

I also happened to have a press tool. It was one of those bolt together tools, along with a bunch of press sleeves, which allowed me to make an "I" termination in some wire that I had onboard. The wire was actually taken from a lifting bridle, which is used to lift a boat out of the water. I fabricated two those two lanyards and attached them to the head stay chain plate. Then I pulled the head stay down as much as I could and clamped the two lanyards onto the existing head stay.

I also used a whole bunch of U-shaped cable clamps, which have a little U-bolt and little saddle, in order to bolt the whole thing together. There are about six of those little things on there.

We sailed about 900 miles to windward with this fix in place, and it served us just fine. So here's one place of where we can learn a lesson of how to recover from a broken chain plate, or a broken terminal, or a failure of any of the component, in the rigging system. It's possible to make a termination from some other material and then clamp it onto the wire and then proceeding on the trip instead of having to turn around and go back home.

We did replace this temporary fix after sailing about 900 miles though. I called a friend of mine back in the States and asked him to have a new chain plate manufactured and sent to me in Hawaii. Then I picked it up when we got back to Hawaii. The failure had taken place when we were sailing in Tonga, on a really wonderful three-week trip around the Lao Islands, which are to windward of the rest of the island chain. Those islands aren't frequented by yachts, so it was really a very special trip. I wasn't going to interrupt it because of that component failure.

Some sailors might not have been able to handle this failure the way I did. There are two aspects to component failure. The first is avoiding them to begin with. If you can possibly find a component that is imminently going to fail and replace it then that is best. The other aspect is taking along enough replacement parts that you can build replacement pieces and clamp them in place, should a failure occur. I had foreseen the possibility of this type of failure on my trip, and, therefore, had materials on board that I could use in order to install a temporary fix. I was sure glad I did at the time too!

Hidden Component Corrosion...
The next image here shows a chain plate, taken from a monohull, but it illustrates one thing. It shows that the part of the chain

plate you cannot see is very possibly the part of the chain plate that is going to fail.

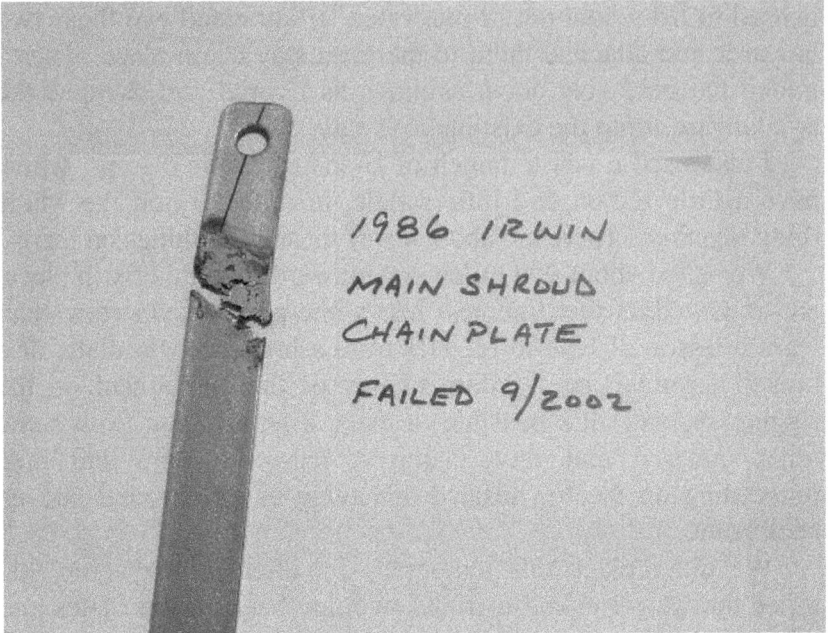

I took this off a boat in 2002. The boat was built in 1986, so it was 16 years old. Chain plates should last longer than 16 years, in my opinion. But what is significant here is this chain plate was bolted to a bulkhead down below. It's a rather long chain plate, and the bottom end of it extends a couple of feet down there with a bunch of holes in it. The portion that is damaged is actually the portion that was hidden by the deck.

This chain plate was on a fiberglass boat, which had plywood coring in the deck. The whole thickness of the deck was about an inch. The chain plate itself was about an inch wide. We can see that it looked beautiful above the deck, and it looked beautiful below the deck. There was very little indication of what was really going on though. What is significant here is the line I've drawn on the upper portion of the chain plate illustrates the line of the shroud that was attached to it.

We see that the shroud is not lined up with the chain plate. That caused one edge of the chain plate (obviously, the left-hand edge of it), to be loaded more highly than the right-hand edge. By examining this failure, we can actually see that the failure started on the left-hand edge and proceeded toward the right-hand edge.

I was actually onboard this particular boat when its chain plate failed. We were out sailing with some friends. In fact, I was steering at the time. All of a sudden, the shroud, attached to the chain plate top, was suddenly dangling in the breeze. I said, *"Uh-oh, we've had a chain plate failure."* So we dropped all the sails and motored back to the dock. Had we not seen it, and tacked over, then we'd have lost the mast.

This chain plate was actually rather small for the size of the boat. It was thin, and it wasn't very wide. The boat it happened to be used on wasn't a high-priced keel boat. It really was known to be a more inexpensive brand. The broken chain plate was very typical of one used by this sort of manufacturer, on other boats that I've seen. Sometimes they actually fiberglass the chain plate into the hull laminate itself, rather than use bolts or anything. If installed that way, the chain plates really are difficult to replace. A boat owner would have to go in with a grinder in order to get it out. This chain plate was bolted in to a bulkhead. But chain plates should be large enough for the duty they're assigned. Chain plates should be lined up with the shroud properly, so the entire width of the chain plate shares the load of the rigging that is attached to it.

On the subject of having a chain plate line up the shroud properly, this something a sailor can see with careful visual inspection. This chain plate was sticking almost straight up through the deck. But the shroud that was attached to it was inclined inboard, just a little bit. It was very obvious when looking at it. In this particular case, there was also a lot of the chain plate sticking up above the deck. As we can seem there looks to be about three inches of it that was standing up above the deck. The hole for this chain plate could have been a lot lower to the deck. It may have prevented such a severe problem. My guess, however, is that the same failure would have eventually occurred. As we see in the picture, the chain plate's stainless steel was coming apart like a French pastry.

What was happening was a combination of oxygen starvation and stress corrosion. This chain plate was under stress, and it was an area in between the top of the deck and the underside of the deck, where it had been caulked in. It had been oxygen-starved and the stainless did not exhibit the corrosion protection that it normally gets by forming chromium oxide on its surface. Then it was placed under stress, which accelerates the corrosion. Any time a piece of metal is under stress, with a standing load on it, will accelerate any corrosion that is occurring.

In the case of this plate, the stress and corrosion worked together in order to create a total failure of this chain plate just 16 years after its installation. If this boat had been surveyed prior to this failure, the only indication of anything possibly going on would be a little rust staining on the chain plate, just on the underside of the deck. But otherwise, the whole thing was beautiful, bright and shiny. It looked wonderful. It almost looked like the day it was put in the boat. This problem was something that was a real sleeper.

The next picture we're going to look at illustrates a far more catastrophic situation. The chain plate on the left is a main shroud chain plate for a Searunner 31 sailing trimaran. It is exhibiting signs of oxygen starvation in the area of those lower bolt holes. We can see the chain plate has broken right across those two lower bolt holes. This plate had been secured on the inside the boat. It was sandwiched between the boat side and a washer. There was oxygen starvation going on, however, in addition to cracking from stress.

On the right-hand side, we see the top end of a lower shroud chain plate from the same boat. It had a doubler welded on the top of it, which was not un-common to see at one time. It's not so common anymore because many sailors now understand that welding on chain plates can cause all sorts of problems. In this instance, the upper end of the chain plate had been thickened up to better support the loads of the pin connecting the rigging. And in so doing, the welding went over the edges.

The piece on the left-hand side was flopped over on top and welded around the edges. It's like the chain plate on the left, the big wide one, which has a doubler on the top. Well, what happens in this case is that a crevice is created in there. We can see there is some rusting going on in there. The crevice has created a situation in which is oxygen starved in that area of the plate, and that started corrosion to the point where, actually, a whole chunk of the top of the chain plate came off. There are actually some pieces of it missing; they're just not there anymore. They've just totally corroded away.

I might also mention that these chain plates were made of type 304 stainless steel. The type of stainless we recommend is 316. It has a higher chromium content, and it's not quite a strong, but you can adjust the thickness of the chain plate to account for that. But it has a much higher corrosion resistance than the 304.

Chain plates are usually made big and heavy. We like for them to be beyond any shadow of a doubt that they're going to carry the load that they're assigned to carry. It's important for sailors to realize that, over time, the strength of chain plates will degrade. And if they're being bent back and forth, just even slightly, they also go through a fatiguing problem that decreases their strength.

The fatiguing in stainless steel makes it much harder and brittle. It then breaks like a chocolate bar. If we exclude oxygen from the stainless, it suffers oxygen starvation corrosion. If we weld it, it totally changes the composition of the metal in the weld area and creates an internal electrical galvanic stress between the grains. What happens is the carbon in the steel migrates through the grain boundaries and then creates a different type of material that self-destructs over a long period of time because of electrolysis within the material. But it also allows a whole bunch of ferrous stuff to come to the surface, which then turns rusty.

The chain plate here has been passivated, which means dipped in a mild solution of sulfuric acid, which burns all the ferrous stuff off the surface, leaving pure chrome. So the stainless becomes nice and bright, but it doesn't change what happened below the surface, which is the real thing that damaged the stainless.

I guess what I'm working up to here is that stainless isn't the wonderful stuff we once thought it was when we first started using it. We've learned a lot about it over time. And 316 stainless is not immune to these same problems, but it's far more resistant to these main problems. Any boat that has had stainless steel chain plates bolted to it for more than ten years probably ought to undergo some significant scrutiny.

If the chain plates on a boat happen to go through the deck of a boat, then they probably ought to be removed and inspected before being replaced. If there was any indication that the types of corrosion we're now talking about here are happening, then those chain plates should probably be totally replaced with new ones. Chain plates are not forever with a boat. Figure on replacing them at some point, and always keep your eye on them.

Other Potential Issues...

The next photo is one we've seen in a previous chapter. This is a chain plate with a whole bunch of stuff attached to it. We see a shroud attached to it. The face of the toggle there is apparent. We also see a pin. (Even the pin looks a little rusty.) The turnbuckle is covered up with a cover, which could be hiding all sorts of other ills. The owner of this boat needs to pull that cover up once in a while and have a look in there and see if there is anything going wrong.

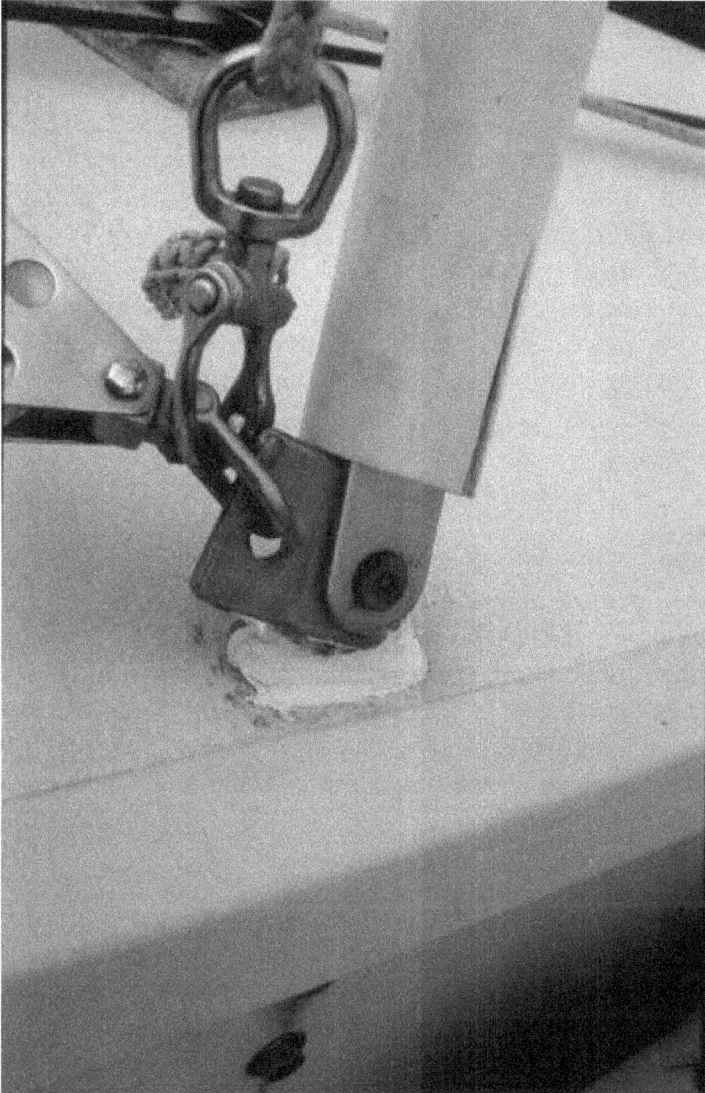

But the possibly worst thing here is another piece of equipment, which is pulling on this chain plate in a different direction. As we can see, someone has attached a block to the chain plate. That snap shackle is probably a halyard, just sitting there lazily at the moment. But if something pulls on that block, it's going to pull the chain plate sideways, which the chain plate wasn't designed to do.

It's pretty obvious that problem is already developing because goopy sealant has already been applied around that chain plate.

Water is probably already leaking underneath it. This chain plate needs to have a chain plate cover, which is a metal plate with a slot, which slides over the top of it. You can buy them down at the local yacht shop or make yourself; it just takes a little time. A chain plate cover would be screwed down to the deck where that sealant currently is, and would work to stop the leakage of water going down through the deck. It would also help stop the corrosion of the chain plate to begin with.

In our photo, we can also see bolts on the hull side there. They look a little bit too rusty. There is something going on there too. There are streaks of rust coming down those bolts. Those bolts should be stainless steel; they should look brighter than what we're seeing in the picture.

The abundance of visual evidence for problems going on here are enough justification for the owner of this boat to pull that chain plate out, inspect the bolts, inspect the chain plate itself and then remove the block from it in order to install the block somewhere else, using another piece of equipment that is properly designed to take the sort of loads what are imposed upon it. That chain plate should just be connected to the rigging wire that it was designed to hold.

The next image here shows three swaged terminals. The upper one there is an attempt to show us what has happened to the wire.

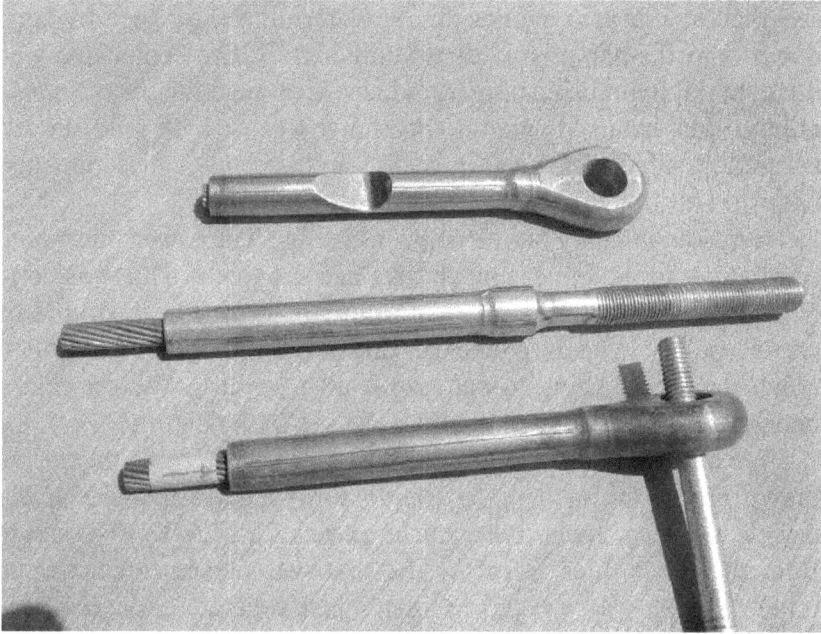

The wire, the cable, has been cut off rather short. We can see just a little bit of stub of the cable hanging out at the left-hand end there. I ground this thing down and polished it up to the point where we can see that the terminal has been squeezed down onto the wire ... it has become pretty much one with the wire itself.

If we look very closely, we can see a few little black dots in there. That's the space in between the wires in the lay of the cable; they're not very big. Terminals like these are very common. It's called a marine eye ... a swaged marine eye terminal.

They're the least expensive of any terminal that you can put on the end of a piece of cable, so they're popular. This is an old one. It was made out of 304 stainless steel, so it's showing a little bit of corrosion. It was going to last for a long time. And it's worth much more than the strength of the cable itself. It'll take the full breaking load of the cable.

The center one is a stud terminal. It receives the top end of the turnbuckle so that the sailor doesn't need another pin and toggle in there. It goes straight into the turnbuckle. These stud terminals are also a favorite piece of equipment that sailors like to use.

Unlike the one above it, which has some lines on it, we can see that in the area where this stud terminal has been swaged down onto the cable is nice and polished. The center one was done by a hydraulic swager, which is a machine that rotates around and bangs down on the thing with a hydraulic die all around ... very fast, very noisy ... and creates a nice polished barrel on it.

It makes it easily for us to inspect this. The lower one was a companion to the upper one and we can see lines. This was done with a swager that had a closing die. It looks like a couple of partial pulley wheels squeezed down on the thing and rolled down the whole thing to squeeze it all together. We see that a bunch of times; it created the lines we see in the picture.

We can see that there is a piece of tape on the cable there; I've drawn an arrow on it. And if we follow the arrow down the barrel, we see a crack. It's a hairline crack. It's hardly discernible from the other lines from the die that was closed down on the thing when it was swaged. But it's just separate enough where we can see it.

This is the sort of thing a good marine surveyor is looking for. It's very common, in these types of terminals, which have been used in a seawater environment, on a boat. I believe that this terminal, at this point, was about 12 years old. Of course, we replaced it. But I've shown a picture of it here to illustrate the sort of things we're looking for. In this case, it was that dark hairline crack.

When I go aboard a boat to survey it, I carry some sandpaper – 600 grit, wet or dry sandpaper. It's very fine stuff. I just polish up barrels like these and take all the rusty streaks off in order to make it nice and bright and shiny. At that point, hairline cracks like these just jump right out at you.

This crack, as we can see, progresses down what looks to be about a third of the way down the barrel that's been swaged ... at the point there where it's been deformed. At that point, if you pull-tested it, it would probably still come right on up to the full strength of the cable. This thing is not in danger of pulling off the end of the cable and causing a failure of the wire assembly right now. It's still got a lot of inherent strength, but that crack is growing. It will eventually proceed down the full length of the barrel.

Part of the reason this crack occurred is that it's impossible to stop water from getting into the wire and proceeding down inside that barrel. Just like the chain plates we previously looked at, it has oxygen starvation going on in there. And that oxygen starvation creates some rust. The rust is a larger molecule. Ferrous oxide is a larger molecule than the steel it comes from, so it tends to expand out. It will cause an expansion of that whole area, and then finally, the failure will occur because the elasticity of the swaged material has just been exceeded. Basically speaking, it's blowing it up. It's expanding to the point where something is going to fail.

The barrel is probably going to fail firs, but the problem is proceeding down the barrel. At this point, it's an absolute requirement that this be replaced. The reason why this while rig hasn't fallen down is that it's still got quite a bit of inherent strength.

How long will this rig last if this problem isn't resolved? Who knows! I used to go around my own boat and look at every one of my terminals before making a passage, making sure that I had as much reliability in all those fittings that I could possibly have by just visually checking them.

Components Breaking...

Then next thing we're going to talk about now is running rigging. What we're looking at in this next picture is a very common block. It is made by a popular manufacturer. But what we're going to be looking at here is that shackle, on the left-hand end of the block. The shackle attaches to the fitting that secures the block, wherever it is.

This particular block was used as a spinnaker halyard block on this boat, so that shackle was wrapped over a bale that was a piece of stainless steel rod about 3/8" in diameter. It's a little hard to see in this photograph, but there is some deformation that has occurred in this shackle. The significant thing is that the manufacturer has quite nicely stamped their name right across the top of the shackle. And we can probably guess that that name stamped in there is not doing anything good for the strength of the shackle.

Let's go to the next photograph. Here is the same block. We can see the deformation that has occurred in that shackle there. We can see that there is really some working of the metal going on there.

In other words, this thing is probably going to break. In fact, this is one of two blocks that were on the same mast, at the same time. The other block did break ... in the middle of the Trans Pac race that I was participating in, while sailing my boat here.

When the break occurred, we dropped the spinnaker, right in front of the boat, and the boat went through it at about 15 knots. We lost that spinnaker, of course, so we had to put up another one, and that other one was attached to this particular block. Thankfully, it held for the rest of the race. But I removed this block after the race. It was, in fact, a brand new block. It was almost brand new at the time of this race. So we can see what occurred in a very, very short period of time.

The shackle that I'm showing at the bottom of our previous picture -- the screw pin shackle that is below the block -- is what should replace the sheet metal shackle that's on the block.

In almost any circumstance, if you buy one of these blocks and it has one of those sheet metal shackles in there, take it off right away. Find one of these big, hunky wire shackles that go on there with a round section. They are so much stronger. They've got about the same amount of "middle" in them, but they're so much stronger than those sheet metal shackles.

This is one way to prevent failures on the boat. If this block was on a genoa sheet lead, or something of that sort, and the genoa sheet lead was taking a big angle, and that thing broke, one might end up wearing that block in their teeth. Some failures can be extremely dangerous onboard a boat because the loads are extremely high.

Preventing these sorts of failures, before they happen, can much improve safety aboard a vessel. Just to illustrate this point, on the next photo here, we can see there are a number of lines on this boat.

We can see a main sheet tackle, right in the foreground here. We don't see the block it's attached to. But we can just imagine what would happen to the main sheet if this were to break. It would probably fling over and the boom would smack the lower shroud. And if that didn't damage the boom, or break it, it might damage the lower shroud.

Something else may also occur. There is a genoa block that is attached just above the horseshoe life preserver that we see. If that thing breaks and somebody was on the deck right in front of it, it could cause a significant amount of bodily harm. A real nasty wound or broken limb could result.

If the block on the outboard ama broke, there would be a good chance that one of those lines might hit a crew member or something else. The bottom line is that every one of these components has to be very reliable.

138

A sailor has to think about whether every component on the boat is big enough to do what it is supposed to do. And they've got to think about whether each of the components has been made well enough to withstand the use that they're going to get.

You've got to think about whether the shackles, and things they're attached to, are not only strong enough, but properly secured to stop thing from coming apart while the boat is underway. You don't want lots of things letting go, for example, just because a pin falls out. That type of thing has happened often on multihulls. So a sailor should always have a look around their boat, understand the equipment they're using, and see whether or not they think all components are in good condition for the next trip out on the water.

Component Water Corrosion...

In the next photograph here, we're looking at the base of a mast. We see a whole bunch of blocks attached to the base of the mast. They all have big shackles.

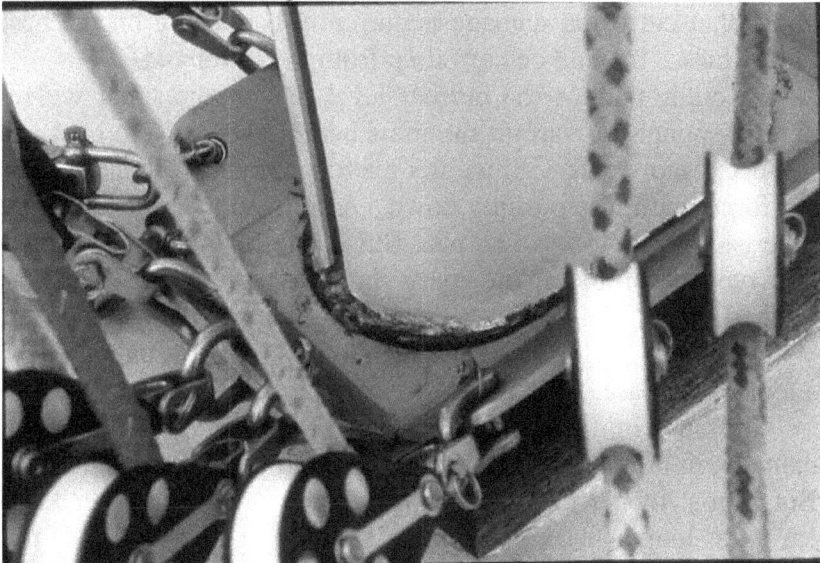

These blocks, however, all use little sheet metal shackles. I don't know why all of those weren't replaced with D shackles. That's one problem here. Another thing we're seeing is corrosion around the base of the mast, which is not uncommon to see. This mast may not have a drain in it.

A lot of these lines in the picture are coming from internal halyards, where the halyards dip into the mast and then go inside the mast, all the way up to the top, and finally come out at the top. When this type of situation occurs, there is a place for water to get in at the top of the mast from rain or sea spray. Sometimes that will cause to water accumulate in the butt of the mast. One may not think it would, but it does.

A friend of mine was doing some work on a boat one day, putting a new cleat on the mast, about six feet up from the base of the mast. He was standing on deck and had a drill. After drilling a hole, he removed the drill and water started peeing out of the mast.

He was very surprised. He thought, *"Man, this thing is full of water!"* So he drilled a hole in the bottom of the mast to let all the water out ... not a very big hole, but water came out of it for about 20 minutes.

If you get a situation like that then you're going to be hoping that it's fresh water coming out. Sea water will do a lot of corrosion damage on the inside of a mast. We can see in our photo that corrosion damage is currently happening on the base of this mast. It could be corroding from the inside out.

I wouldn't judge the current level of corrosion that we see here is enough to warrant the mast being taken off the boat and inspected more fully. Since the mast is a compression member, the force upon it is pushing down. A little corrosion at the mast base isn't really too dangerous. But if one finds ever encounters this type of problem, the mast should should be cleaned and washed. And if a boat owner is doing any major work on the boat, then it is probably a good idea to pull the mast out and have a look at the base.

The base might need to be shored up a bit if there is any damage, in order to build the base back up to where it should be. But a boat owner can recover from this sort of situation fairly easily, as long as the corrosion isn't extensive. The owner of this boat would certainly want to make sure this mast has a drain inside of it to drain water out. And if they're going to keep the boat for any length of time, the mast really needs to be washed down in order to get rid of all the accumulation of chlorides (salt) out of there. Salt is a very corrosive element for any kind of metal.

I used to work in the aerospace business. My company sold products that were going on spacecraft, to be launched into space. One problem that was discovered was that such products often had to spend quite a bit of time at Cape Kennedy before actually being launched into space aboard the spacecraft. Manufacturers discovered that the Cape Kennedy area was a very corrosive environment. We had to put our products through salt spray testing in order to test their resistance to corrosion. Just three weeks' worth of salt spray testing in a chamber would reduce the most beautiful looking hardware to absolute junk. It was quite surprising how severe salt is within an environment.

For this reason, keeping the boat clean, including washing all areas off, wherever possible, in order to get rid of accumulated salt, goes a long way towards stopping corrosion from happening on boat hardware.

Winch Without Maintenance...

The next photograph here shows a winch. It looks like a bird got in there and pooped everywhere. That is aluminum oxide.

This particular boat had been in passenger service. For some reason, it appears that, for several years, the way the sailors had rigged the passenger service meant this winch never had to be used. It's one of the main winches on the boat, but apparently the jib never got sheeted in on this side of the craft.

I am guessing that the sailors always traveled the same way. They left the harbor, went sailing for a while, and then came back. But somehow, that winch was never used. By the time I arrived to survey this boat, this winch almost wouldn't rotate without the use of a wrench. After pulling the winch apart, this is what we found.

Let's talk about winches for a moment. Winches are constructed out of so many different kinds of metal; one wonders why they don't corrode away more easily than they do. The base of this winch in our picture, including the centerline shaft sticking up there, is made of bronze. That's the way most winches are constructed. The roller bearings that actually perform the load for the drum are stainless steel. We can see one of them, right there left on the shaft, and there's another one that is up inside the drum that didn't want to come out.

The drum itself is made of aluminum. Aluminum drums are much more preferable to bronze drums because when you wrap a line around the winch and give it a yank, the winch spins up easily because the drum is fairly lightweight. If it were a bronze drum, this winch would probably weigh three times as much, and every time a line is put on it, an awful lot of energy I spent just trying to spin the drum in order to yank the line to pull the sheet. So aluminum winches are not only lighter, they're much easier to use. Almost everyone will have a preference for aluminum drum winches.

One caveat here is that they need yearly greasing. You've got to take aluminum winches apart every year and grease them. They're usually easy to pop apart, but there are different manufacturers and different ways they can come apart. There is usually a snap ring, or screw, or something on the top, and you can take it out and then take the whole thing apart, piece by piece. Just put grease on all the bits and check it for corrosion.

This winch drum in our picture was aluminum and it was hard-anodized. Aluminum winches can last for a long time if they're greased. But the anodizing on this winch had corroded away. When aluminum corrodes, it creates a lot of white powder (aluminum oxide). In fact, the aluminum oxide can grow to a significant amount. The white powder grew on the inside of this winch and occupied a lot of space; it really jammed up the winch to the point where it hardly moved. All that white powder had been building up for a long time. This boat had once been a race boat. It was raced to Hawaii and then eventually ended up being put in service as a six-pack sailing charter boat. My guess would be the winch we're talking about here had not been re-greased since it was brand new, off the shelf. The boat was about ten years old when this picture was taken.

Maintaining the hardware on your multihull may include lubrication of certain pieces of equipment. Winches certainly require it. And proper hardware maintenance goes a long way in stopping failures from happening. This winch was an expensive failure. The winch base was okay, but the bearings need replacement. The winch drum needs to be replaced and possibly some of the palls and springs too. But the owner of this boat is probably looking at spending a thousand dollars' worth of replacement parts, at least.

Rudder Coming Apart...

The next photograph we're going to look at is a self-steering auxiliary rudder for a boat. These rudders are common on cruising boats.

Whether or not a wind-vane steers the main rudder, or an auxiliary rudder is used, we are talking about a mechanical gizmo here. I happened to be delivering this particular boat it to the mainland from Hawaii. The assembly of this auxiliary rudder had not been done to the manufacturer's specifications, which called for the use of Locktite on all of the fastenings that held it together. This meant that during our passage, on a daily basis, one of our crew had to go back to the rudder and tighten its bolts, which did not have self-locking nuts.

This rudder had a bunch of slide-together fittings, with set screws in them, which were not put in using Locktite and would come loose all the time. In order to keep this rudder working every day, somebody had to go back there with some tools and put things back together again. The only reason we discovered this problem is because we almost lost the entire rudder one day. It almost fell off the boat.

One of us noticed a piece of it moving around but nothing had been lost at that point. It was on the verge of self-destructing though. Had we lost that self-steering vane, the trip would not have been very nice. One of us would have had to hold onto the wheel constantly. Anyone who has ever ever sailed across an ocean with a wind-vane really gets to like it if the thing is working properly. It allows a sailor to become mostly a passenger on the boat. There is not much to do once a wind-vane is set up for the day, unless the weather changes.

So we can use this situation to illustrate the importance of making sure the hardware on the boat is properly mounted, with proper fasteners, which are going to stay in place and stay tight while the voyage proceeds. Otherwise, you're going to create a lot of maintenance for yourself and possibly lose all fun from the entire trip.

Ventilators Leaking...

The next photograph is one we've seen before. The thing I want to illustrate here is that even with the best intentions, some things go awry.

This was the delivery boat that I brought back (the same boat we've been looking at.) The mushroom ventilator on the top of the hatch is the focus of our discussion here. There were three of us aboard this boat – me, a crew member that I'd hired, and a guy who'd been sent over to prep the boat before its delivery.

Two of us (I and one other crew member) understood that if any leakage occurred with that mushroom ventilator then the bunk underneath it would turn into a swamp. So we gave that berth to the fellow who asked us for it.

It turned out that mushroom ventilator was not properly sealed down to the hatch. We ended up having bad weather along the way and something leaked badly. A lot of rain and spray ended up turning the bunk underneath that ventilator into a mess.

There is a lesson to be learned here. If you put a hatch over a bunk, anywhere in a boat, you've got to make sure that thing is never going to leak. This would have been difficult to do on this boat because the hatch cover itself was made of fiberglass-coated wood, with that plastic skylight piece on top of it. The plastic skylight probably changed shape, more than a 16th of an inch in width and length, due to hot day sun and cold evenings. The sealant used to seal the piece of plastic down to the wood construction has to have a lot of give to it. The only thing that I know can be used is silicone rubber. And then the thing has to be properly bolted down. The skylight requires through bolts (not screws), and those bolts are screwed into over-sized holes, which are dilled on the plastic. This means the hardware is going to move around in there, and if silicone sealant isn't tightening ... or doesn't cure properly ... then there is the possibility of leakage.

Many of these types of installations also use a real rubber gasket, working in conjunction with the sealant. I wrote a little booklet called "Standard Details" that details this sort of thing. It tells boat owners, for example, how they can install windows on a boat properly ... windows that won't leak! Leaks such as this can drive a boat owner crazy.

Fixing Components on a Beach, if Necessary...

The final photograph in this chapter shows one thing multihulls are able to do. It's the one fallback you've got with a multihull. As a multihull owner, if you do have difficulty with the boat, whether it's just an overhead leak, or something below waterline, you can always put the thing on a beach somewhere and fix it on the beach.

You'll usually have enough time, between tides, to put some underwater epoxy or similar product on a problem in order fix a problem, temporarily at least. I've actually made some pretty good repairs between tides when the need arose.

I've also done bottom painting and other routine maintenance on a beach. In our picture, the boat owner is working on a propeller. He is probably replacing the propeller, or changing props, or something like that, on this beach.

I used to do my trimaran's maintenance on a beach, as much as I possibly could. The only places I found it difficult were some places in the tropics, where there wasn't enough tide. In

Tahiti, for example, there is only six inches of tide on a daily basis. It's a sun tide. It goes low at midnight and high at noon. But that's unusual. In Fiji, there was about four feet of tide, so I'd have no problem doing any maintenance on a beach there. In Southern California, we probably had about six feet of tide. San Francisco also had normal tides of about six feet.

The main point here is that a multihull owner has a boat that makes it relatively easy to do one's own maintenance. You can look all over the boat pretty easily and make sure there is nothing cracked, nothing leaking, and just have a good look around to see if anything doesn't look quite right. If you do find anything that doesn't look right then it probably isn't right. You'll want to take time for a little more examination in order to avoid an oncoming component failure. This is key to preventing component failures. Try and figure out what is happening and making necessary changes before things break.

CHAPTER SIX
BENEFITS OF A MARINE SURVEY FOR YOUR MULTIHULL

In this chapter, we're going to talk about the what, why, when and how of multihull surveying. Let's begin by discussing what it means to survey a boat, including a multihull, and why somebody would want to survey their craft.

I've been in the multihull business for 41 years and just had the privilege of surveying my old Searunner 37 trimaran, which was built 41 years ago. My experience shows why surveyors form a portion of the whole marine industry. Most people don't know what a surveyor does or why he does it.

Surveying is often a requirement for administrative reasons. If a boat buyer wants to finance a boat or insure it against damage, for example, then they'll need to get it surveyed so the lender or insurer has a report about the condition of the boat. But I like to look at surveying another way. More than anything else, I believe that a surveyor is an advocate for a boat's owner, or would-be owner.

A multihull is a rather complicated machine. It's sort of a combination between a house and maybe an airplane. It has a lot of technology in it that needs to be a part of the boat for specific reasons. There are guidelines and standards that need to be followed as part of its construction and maintenance. And there are compliance requirements that must be adhered to for Coast Guard regulations. What a surveyor does is look at a boat, inspect it, and see how it complies in relation to all of the various requirements. In the end, it attempts to answer the real question as to whether the boat is fit to perform the duty for which it was designed.

Used Boats, New Boats & Potential Problems...

My old Searunner trimaran ... the one I recently surveyed ... has been sailed for tens of thousands of miles over its lifespan. That's pretty amazing because I was very young when I built it, so the boat shows the level of understanding for the materials used for home-built boats at the time. But I and some friends sailed that trimaran in the 1972 Trans Pac Race. After Trans Pac, my wife and I did a two-year, 20,000 mile circuit through the

South Pacific and returned back to the west coast of California. So this Searunner has some miles on it and there are some lessons to be learned from it.

Self-builders have access to much better materials for boatbuilding nowadays. Modern wooden boats are expected to last a lot longer. But seeing my old boat, still going after 41 years, still able to do an ocean passage … that isn't too bad.

My survey opportunity came about because the boat was being sold to its 3ʳᵈ owner. I got a call to do a survey of the boat just prior to its sale, which is the time you want to call a professional marine surveyor. As a matter of fact, the time to call a surveyor is anytime you're ready to buy any boat, including a *brand new* one. It's just as important to hire a marine surveyor to inspect a brand new boat as a used one. I've surveyed new boats on the shipping dock, right from the manufacturer, and found significant deficiencies.

Most people would never suspect that a new boat coming to them directly from the factory could have significant problems, but that that is the case. One has to understand that a factory is interested in producing boats and getting them out the door. Their quality assurance may not be up to the level of an airplane manufacturer. Some factory boat builders just push their products out the door as fast as possible. Oftentimes, there are subpar processes and installations.

Having the boat surveyed on the dock, after it arrives, while adding a little cost to the purchase price, is something every new boat owner should do, in my opinion. Your surveyor may find a significant number of things that need to be fixed by the manufacturer. At that point, your surveyor has probably paid for himself or herself. If you don't get a boat surveyed when buying it, then when you want to sell it yourself, you may end up having to pay for deficiencies the manufacturer should have taken care of when you bought that boat brand new. So it pays to hire a surveyor.

A surveyor can serve as a second set of eyes for you. Installations originally performed on the boat are done by technicians in the factory. Sometimes those technicians are in a hurry to leave on Friday afternoon and they forget things. A good surveyor can go inside your boat and uncover them. If a surveyor ends up doing that then they've done the sort of work they're supposed to do.

What a Surveyor Must Inspect...

Whenever I survey a boat, what I'm trying to do, first of all, is assess the soundness of all the surfaces on the craft. I inspect the hulls, including hull bottoms, sides, decking, joints and cabin. Then I examine all of the individual installations that are included for that particular boat. I actually go over the structure with a hammer, which might sound sort of brutal, but it's a plastic hammer. I do that in order to listen to how things sound by tapping around the surfaces. If there is any softness to wood or other building material, it will make a different sound. Some surveyors use other non-destructive methods to investigate, such as moisture meters. I personally feel that moisture meters give enough false negatives that surveyors who use them spend as much time explaining those false negatives as explaining readings that are actually worthwhile.

Most of the boats I've survey are wood. Most new ones, of course, are plastic. But basically, a surveyor is looking for structural soundness. We're also looking for compliance with regards to electrical guidelines and standards. We look for anything that affects the safety of operation of the vessel. If a surveyor is lucky, they'll get to survey a boat in the rain. Rain will often reveal where leaks are, which may not be evident unless it's raining.

In brand new boats, I've found, for instance, significant gel coat deficiencies, right on the delivery dock. I've discovered blisters underneath the gel coat after tapping on them. The gel coat just broke away and revealed huge, huge blisters. Such blisters are what some surveyors call "neverbonds," meaning the materials were never really glued together. Perhaps the fiberglass matrix was not pressed down onto the gel coat finish properly. Something like that would cause a bubble in that area. It's easy to repair a small blister with a bit of putty that is the same color as the hull. But that blister goes undetected for a number of years, before breaking through the gel coat, and then it can be an expensive repair. The owner will have to pull the boat out of the water and perform the repair at their own expense.

With older boats, there are often electrical deficiencies, due to improvements in electrical specifications. It's very common. In the old days, a lot of boats had electrical wiring that was a combination of AC and DC systems. They had shore power coming on board, and the third wire, the green wire in the AC system, was hooked directly to the DC ground system in the boat. That type of thing can be fatal in a number of ways. For one thing, if there is any mistake or any electrical problem in the boat, the boat may end up emitting 110 volts into the water around the craft, which can be life-threatening to nearby swimmers. It might also mean that any stray currents will cause the zinc anodes, which protect underwater metal parts, to erode very quickly. If that happens then the metal parts themselves begin to corrode. It can mean potential for shock hazards onboard the boat from ungrounded appliances. So inspection of the electrical system is very necessary.

Another thing a marine survey can detect is the danger of the boat actually sinking. I've seen underwater plumbing that really was not fit to be used without somebody standing there watching it all the time. I am speaking here about hoses connected to through-hulls. There's one manufacturer that uses a spiral-type hose, generally used in bilge pump systems, below the water line. And this spiral hose can't be connected directly to a hose bar because it has a texture to it. So they glue to a rubber cuff on the end, which has a smooth texture, so it can fit down over a hose barb, where clamps can then be put on it. The problem is that even though the manufacturer has clamped the cuff, the glued-on hose is merely glued in place while being under pressure with seawater, all the time. If that glue ever fails then the boat will sink. That is the type of situation most boat owners would never know about.

One general thing I look for is the prevalent use of vinyl hoses on boats being connected to through-hull fittings below the water line. Such vinyl hoses are fine for the onboard water system. But I really don't think it's a good idea to use them on through-hull fittings below the water line. There are no standards against it at the moment. But I know for a fact that it's possible to put a piece of vinyl hose on a hose barb, tighten the clamp, walk away, and then tomorrow, come back and pull that hose right off the hose barb. It loosens ups. Vinyl is not like rubber, which maintains a squeeze onto the hose barb. It actually cold flows away and loosens up. So this is all an example of the sorts of things your surveyor should inspect.

A Surveyor That Knows Multihulls...

Experience plays a large part in how any marine survey approaches things. Some surveyors are better than others. All surveyors are not equal, and all surveyors do not know about multihulls. Anybody wanting to find a surveyor for their catamaran, trimaran or proa is well advised to go find one with expertise in multihulls. Ask them immediately if they're a candidate. You can always just call a surveyor up and ask if they know about multihulls. If they say, *"Yes,"* then ask, *"What is your experience working with multihulls?"* Some surveyors will tell you, right off the bat, *"Gee, I wouldn't even sail one of those things across a mud puddle."* Someone like that obviously wouldn't be a good choice for the person you want to hire to be an inspector of your multihull.

Multihulls are now an accepted portion of the established yachting world. So more surveyors are familiar with these types of boats nowadays than have ever been in the past.

I've been asked to give seminars for other marine surveyors on how to properly survey a multihull. A few years ago, I gave a talk at the meeting of the National Association of Marine Surveyors (NAMS) about multihulls. There were quite a number of surveyors in that group who knew very little about multihulls, and my intention was to basically try and familiarize them with the "multihull animal."

Multihulls are different from keel boats. They have very different loads. They have very different failure mechanisms. Surveyors should know about these differences.

In some cases, surveys are required to access a boat for insurance reasons. They're always required for financial reasons; the most obvious one is financing a boat purchase. If there's any damage to a boat, from being run into by another boat, for example, an insurance company will want a surveyor to inspect the boat before loaning out money for its purchase.

In addition to the preceding circumstances, a person simply may have a boat they're familiar with, but also have questions about its current condition. They may see some cracks occurring somewhere, or they want to make some sort of structural modification, or something like that. For them, a multihull expert or multihull surveyor can probably help on a consulting basis. Such a person may not need a full survey performed that results in a full report. A multihull owner might just need some consulting time in order to get important questions answered.

I personally do this a lot, and for boats that are far different from any of my designs. Sometimes a boat owner just wants to make a few changes because certain circumstances arise as a result of change in boat's ownership. The new owner may want to add new things onto an older vessel they've just bought but they need some professional input first. I've surveyed boats that have had incredible mistakes made in previous modifications to it that really caused some structural deficiencies. Modifications are not something any boat owner should approach lightly. There are experts out there they can talk to. Anybody contemplating a modification to their boat should really talk to an expert first.

How to Preserve the Value of Your Boat Using a Surveyor...

A surveyor should be hired or consulted anytime a boat is purchased, sold, or modified. The person who purchases the boat is the one that pays for the survey. He or she is the one who is going to assume ownership of the craft, whether it is new or used. They are going to need a survey, first of all, if they want to buy insurance for it. And they may be required to hire a surveyor for other financial reasons. But more than anything else, he or she will want to know what the current value and condition of the boat is. And that's really what a survey is all about.

A survey is an inspection of the boat for the purpose of determining its condition and value. They are called "C&D Surveys." The condition is the most important thing. Obviously, a person buying a used boat wants to make sure that the boat is not going to immediately require a lot of maintenance cost. Many boats are sold "as is," and the current owner has no interest in bringing it up to a current specification to make it comply with all of the standards that apply today that didn't apply when the boat was built. So the new owner might be looking at a significant cost to bring the boat up to current specs. It's important for them to make an assessment of what that cost might be. They need to know the severity of the upgrades and repairs that are required. This is the purpose of the survey.

I certainly understand that if a boat's monetary value is under $10,000 then a person is probably just go and buy it without getting a survey. An insurance company may even insure a boat like that without requiring a survey. But even in a case like that, a surveyor would be able to tell the one who wants to buy the boat whether it is in good condition or not. If the surveyor is familiar with the design then they may be able to give the prospective buyer a good idea about how the boat sails, if the would-be owner has never sailed a boat like it before.

Some boat designs are known to be poorer performers under sail than others. Other types of boats don't really accommodate a certain number of people very well. I can name a number of designers who designed really beautiful boats. If you saw one of their designs in an anchorage, you'd think, "*Wow, that's really a nice looking boat!*" But if you got onboard and went down below, you'd find out that the living accommodations, including ergonomics and various spaces, really weren't very well laid out for the convenience of passengers.

I've seen interior designs that are very awkward, or too small, or caused everyone to bump their head all of the time because the overhead was low. There are often compromises made against making a boat comfortable in order to make it beautiful. This is especially the case in boats between 25 and 40 feet long. Boats over 50 feet long tend to look fairly low and sleek regardless of the size of the persons who will be fitting inside the boat. But smaller boats with cabin structures force the boat's designer to choose between drawing a cabin structure that is comfortable, on the one hand, or one that is aesthetically pleasing, on the other hand. A comfortable cabin may appear to be over-sized, thus detracting from the aesthetics. A designer's problem is always to make a boat look nice, plus make it accommodate people well. A surveyor might be able to give a prospective boat owner insight about these particular issues.

There are two main organizations that certify surveyors. One is NAMS, the National Association of Marine Surveyors. The other one is SAMS which stands for, Society of Accredited

Marine Surveyors. Both of these organizations have certification levels that start with "associate" and go up to "certified."

Each can be found on the web. NAMS is *www.namsglobal.org* and SAMS is *www.marinesurvey.org*. There are a few independent surveyors still out there. Most of them would probably be doing only insurance work or that sort of thing. It's also possible to call any number of recognized boat designers on the phone and ask them if they might be able to recommend any good marine surveyors. If you called up a boat designer who lives in your area then you might be able to ask them if they can specifically recommend a good local marine surveyor that lives nearby.

Ideally, you'll want to hire a surveyor who possesses a high level of competence and trust within the multihull community. I mostly work on the East coast because I now live in Maine. But I've gone all over the country to do surveys because the people hiring me felt that they wanted me specifically for their job. But if people called me for recommendations of surveyors in a particular area of the country then I'll certainly give them a referral if I can. Otherwise, NAMS and SAMS are good places to start. Just be sure to call the surveyor up and ask what they think about multihulls. Ask them if they've surveyed the particular type of boat that you're looking at. Try and get some sort of a feeling if they have a bias for or against multihulls and then what their experience level is in relation to having surveyed multihulls in the past.

Don't be afraid to ask questions, especially if you're the one who is going to be paying for them to do work for you. Keep in mind that if you're paying for a surveyor then their working for you. You are paying for them to be your advocate, even if the survey is required by the insurance company for insurance purposes. The surveyor should help you by giving a full assessment and list of things that need to be done, if any, in order for the boat to meet compliancy standards and insurability requirements.

www.ingramcontent.com/pod-product-compliance
Lightning Source LLC
Chambersburg PA
CBHW072013040426
42447CB00009B/1615